MISSIONAL MOONSHOTS

INSIGHT AND INSPIRATION
FOR EDUCATIONAL INNOVATION

DR. BERNARD BULL

Missional Moonshots

Insight & Inspiration for Educational Innovation

Dr. Bernard Bull

ATHANATOS
PUBLISHING GROUP

Missional Moonshots: Insight and Inspiration for Educational Innovation
by Bernard Dean Bull

1st ed. ISBN: 978-1-936830-86-2
Copyright © 2016 by Bernard Dean Bull.
www.bernardbull.com
Illustrations by Ksenia Spiring
Illustrations Copyright © 2016 Bernard Dean Bull

Published by Athanatos Publishing Group
www.athanatos.org
Cover by Julius Broqueza
Cover Art Copyright © 2016 Athanatos Publishing Group

Special discounts are available on quantity purchases by corporations, associations, and others. For details, visit www.bernardbull.com.

"Everything that is done in the world is done by hope."
Martin Luther

Table of Contents

Section IV: Knowing and Nurturing Your Personal Practices and Perspectives

Section V: Knowing (or Creating) the Future of Education

Introduction

For those of us who work in the field of education, these are inspiring and exciting times. Yes, we have plenty of challenges, but there are also countless possibilities and opportunities. This is a remarkably colorful era of education, whether we are exploring education in kindergarten through high school (K-12), higher education, or the rapidly growing space of educational experimentation beyond the walls of formal learning organizations.

I once counted more than thirty schooling options for each of my two children within fifteen miles of our home, choices that highlight more than a dozen educational philosophies and distinct emphases. This fact represents a great strength and source of hope in modern and emerging American education.

As I reflect on the current context, I'm especially encouraged by at least five additional features of this age:

Choice and Individual Uniqueness Are Winning

Even as some people are pushing for greater standardization, the current obvious winner in the K-12 level in most states is that of choice and honoring the uniqueness of each young person. Some might argue that our national well-being depends upon producing as many science, technology, engineering, and mathematics (STEM) graduates as possible, but the louder voice in education today recognizes that we are best served by helping every young person discover his or her gifts, talents, abilities, and passions; nurturing and building on those abilities; and helping each person discover how those abilities can be refined, harnessed, and used for personal well-being and service to others.

We generally recognize that the world is not turned into a better place by encouraging young people to abandon their love of music for a job as an electrical engineer or encouraging budding authors to instead pursue the study of medicine. Each person has gifts that can be discovered, opened, and used through quality education. Leaving the gifts of some people unrecognized and unopened simply results in a world with fewer gifts to celebrate. Most people support an education system that is a mass gift opening and a sharing of those gifts with the world.

Those Working in Education Are Largely Champions

As much as I critique dominant practices and policies in formal education, my hope is renewed when I talk to so many people working in education who clearly do not buy into a vision for education as a factory for producing standardized workers. These people include school administrators, teachers, founders of new models of schooling, board members, venture capitalists, people working in the new face of educational publishing and product development, and many educational entrepreneurs. I have no doubt there are people with less than noble motives, but what I see is largely a group of people who want to help provide quality education, increase access and opportunity, and equip learners to thrive in a 21st and 22nd century world.

Yes, there are cynical people in education, but such people are generally not gaining nearly as much attention or traction as the optimistic, innovative, student-centered difference-makers in many aspects of education, especially if we look at what gains the most attention in the digital world. Promise and possibility are what we lift up and celebrate in some of the most recognized spaces and learning organizations today. This is an age of exploring the possibilities and embracing the opportunities.

Education Is So Much More Than Schooling

If we trace public conversations about education over the last five decades, we see that the dominant voices and innovations are largely focused on schooling and on what happens in formal learning organizations. Today, we continue to see promising conversations within schools, but now learning is seen as life-long. Anyone with an Internet connection, confidence, curiosity, and basic skills has access to potentially transformational learning. Mentors and coaches are a click away. Open education resources, online learning communities, and experiments with myriad free or inexpensive online learning resources are spreading around the world. These agents have not removed serious issues related to equity, access, and opportunity, but they provide us with new possibilities for addressing such issues. Education beyond schooling is emerging as a powerful form of social innovation that is gaining attention from the federal government to Silicon Valley, from private investors to grassroots community organizations.

Schools were never designed to monopolize educational opportunities. They play a valuable role, but there is great promise in the fact that our age sees school as one of many valuable sources of learning throughout life. This reality dominates the contemporary education space.

A Shift in Focus from Teaching to Learning

There was a time when conversations about education were focused largely on the delivery of content and the role of teacher, but today the conversation has changed. It is now so much more about learning. Since student learning is the goal, this change in focus gives us great hope. People don't necessarily agree about what should be learned, how it should be learned, how learners might be assessed, or many related topics. Some don't accept the shift toward the learner. Nonetheless, it is a shift, one that prioritizes what is best for students. While there are competing efforts today, at least in the public debate, we live in a time when the public is largely on the side of those arguments framed around what is best for students.

Educational Research and Innovation

Research in the past few decades has given us a wealth of new insights in education, human cognition, human development, and human well-being. Mind-brain education and positive psychology, to name only two fields, give us rich insights into how people learn and how we might best design engaging and powerful learning environments and experiences.

While much of this research has not yet found its way into public conversations about education or even into educational policy forums, the word is getting out. In addition, more of this scholarship is reaching larger audiences through digital and social media, including wildly popular online videos like TED Talks. People may not be deeply informed about the nuances of the research, but many more of those research findings are reaching the public than at any other time in history.

Similarly, with the growth around education startups, we see a new breed of education business that seeks to tap into education research to design products and services that truly work and benefit people in formal and informal learning environments. The exploration and experimentation can sometimes be messy, with plenty of failed experiments, but the sheer number of experiments today is heartening.

Things are certainly not perfect in education. We have big issues to address. Yet, when I reflect on the current landscape, I am hopeful. I see champions for students, advocates for the unique gifts of each person, an expansion from a narrow focus on schooling to a broader understanding of education, and promising educational research and innovation. Even as we tackle the most pressing problems in contemporary education, elements like these can give us encouragement.

Why This Book?

This is a time for creativity and innovation in education. When we blend the spirit of the innovator and the entrepreneur with the passion and conviction of mission-minded education, we have a powerful force. These five features of our current age give us hope and opportunity. For those current and future innovators in our midst, these features are launch pads for our educational moonshots. They are starting points to imagine, create, and innovate.

I wrote this book for people who believe that education in all its forms can be better, that we can imagine and create new possibilities for learning that engage, empower, and extend access and opportunity. I wrote these essays to offer inspiration, insight, and encouragement for educators, learners, parents, educational leaders, community members, policymakers, and anyone else who wants not only to prepare for the future of education, but also to help shape it. It is my hope and prayer that the following essays contribute to educational moonshots that matter.

I've written this text so that you can read it from the beginning to end, or you can pick and choose among the essays that most capture your attention or have immediate relevance to your current work. Essays are short and to the point, each one representing a distinct concept, tip, or issue. At the same time, many of the essays are interconnected, so you will find several themes restated and repeated throughout the book, recognizing that not everyone will read it from the beginning to the end. In some parts, this book might read like an educational equivalent of *Chicken Soup for the Soul*. At other times, it is a collection of practical tips for leading change and innovation. In still other instances, it is an informal survey of theories, philosophies, and research that has relevance for the educational innovator. What holds them together is a persistent focus on the pursuit of mission-minded educational innovation.

The book is divided into five related categories, beginning with "Knowing the Foundations of Missional Innovation," a collection of essays that explores important questions about why we innovate in education and some of the foundational considerations if we want to be successful. The second section, "Knowing the Context and People," looks at the many factors that inform our plans and thinking about the pursuit of a given educational innovation. I give special attention in that section to a series of essays about the different types of stakeholders, their approaches and responses to innovation, and how these insights increase our chances of success. "Knowing Tips and Tricks," the third section, moves into specific ideas on how to promote an innovation in a learning organization, as well as how to nurture a spirit of innovation and entrepreneurship in a learning organization. Following that is a section entitled "Knowing and Nurturing Your Personal Practices and Perspectives" which offers essays to help the individual innovator and educational entrepreneur think about his or her own habits, perspectives, and practices. I share personal examples along with more general advice on how to grow as one who leads and innovates from depth while benefiting from diverse perspectives. The final section, "Knowing (or Creating) the Future of Education," is a small collection of essays that presents ways of thinking about, preparing for, and helping to create the future of education through the mindset of the educational innovator and entrepreneur.

Collectively, these essays are intended as fuel for the fire of missional innovation in education. I wrote them with the hopes of challenging, inspiring, enlightening, and informing. They represent lessons from personal study, research, experimentation, and experience. None of them is intended to be a prescription for success as much as a resource on each reader's unique journey as an educational innovator and entrepreneur.

Section I:
Knowing the Foundations of Missional Innovations

1

On Mission-Driven Innovation

I am a collector. I collect books, ideas, and quotes. I have notebooks full of scribbled quotes from books, articles, lectures, presentations, movies, and songs. Other notes are inspired by random thoughts and experiences. Out of all the quotes and notes, some come to mind regularly, and I welcome them as I would an old friend.

Are You Selling Sugar Water?

One of the most persistent of these regular visitors is, "Do you want to sell sugar water for the rest of your life, or do you want to come with me and change the world?"

These are the words allegedly spoken by Steve Jobs to John Scully, words that convinced Scully to leave his high-level position at Pepsi Cola and take the risk of joining a four-year-old startup called Apple. Each time I read, hear, or remember this quote, I am drawn into a reflection about my own life's work. Am I selling sugar water right now, or am I doing something that can change the world? The quote is a humbling and inspiring reminder to me to take seriously how I choose to spend my time and energy. I challenge you to consider this question for yourself. How you answer it will depend on your talents, abilities, passions and interests, opportunities, life circumstances, and the events around you.

When it comes to educational innovation, such a quote is a reminder that innovation in itself is neither noble or worth the investment of our lives, unless it is innovation that serves something greater.

Choose How You Will Live in the Time You're Given

Another quote that sweetly haunts me from time to time is: "'I wish it need not have happened in my time,' said Frodo. 'So do I,' said Gandalf, 'and so do all who live to see such times. But that is not for them to decide. All we have to decide is what to do with the time that is given us.'"

From J.R.R. Tolkien's *The Fellowship of the Ring*, this short exchange between Gandalf and Frodo speaks to what we can't change. We don't get to choose the time or place into which we are born. We don't get to choose many of the challenges, troubles, or world events that will occur during our lives. All we can choose is how we will live in those times and how we will or will not respond to them.

Have the Courage of Esther

Here's another from the book of Esther: "For if you remain silent at this time, relief and deliverance for the Jews will arise from another place, but you and your father's family will perish. And who knows but that you have come to your royal position for such a time as this?"

These words were spoken to Queen Esther by her cousin Mordecai, who had learned of the evil plot to destroy all of the Jews in Persia on a certain date. Esther, a Jew herself, might have believed she would be safe since she was married to the king, but Mordecai warned her that she, too, was in danger and in this quote urged her to use her position as queen to save her people. Queen Esther had to decide whether she would stand by silently while her people were massacred or speak to the king on their behalf, even at the risk of her own life.

This quote calls me to consider the opportunity and purpose behind the circumstances in my life. Regardless of my life's circumstances, it drives me to ask myself,

"Could it be that I am here for such a time as this?"

Respect the Risks

The following quote is from Jim Shelton, who spoke these words to a group at the 2012 *Education Innovation Summit*: "Most revolutions end with the people still oppressed by the same or a different cruel master."

These words, spoken in the context of educational innovation, remind me that we must undertake our work toward educational innovation with a solemn respect for the risks that work entails. There is a very real danger that our solutions to one problem or oppressor will only create a new problem or oppressor, and it is often difficult for us to foresee such things.

Remain True to that Which Is Constant

And this one, from William Ralph Inge: "Whoever marries the spirit of this age will find himself a widower in the next."

Inge's quote is a humbling reminder not to become attached to those things that are fleeting, but rather to remain true to those things that are constant across time and generations. I do not interpret this quote to mean that we should ignore all trends and innovations, but it does drive us to strive for a clear and compelling reason before we follow the next new trend. What is the larger goal, purpose, or value? I will return to this concept in a moment.

Applying These Powerful Words to Our Work

One important thing that we can do before venturing into educational innovation is to make sure that we have depth, meaning, and purpose in our innovations. We do not innovate because innovation itself is inherently admirable, but because innovation helps us to pursue promising opportunities in education and to address critical challenges and needs. Education is a field that, at its foundation, is about social good. We want to pursue innovation that matters, innovation that is shaped and informed by that which is true, good, beautiful, or admirable.

What matters is that we innovate from something solid. While the following questions overlap, each one provides a different way of thinking about the foundations of our educational innovations. Consider using one or more of these questions both individually and in your learning organization to discover or nurture a core that will inspire your innovation and keep you focused amid life's distractions.

What Is Your Calling?

In the late 1940s and early 1950s, a college student explored what he wanted to do with his life. He started his studies at Dartmouth College but later graduated from a small college in Florida with a degree in music composition. He had a love of music and children, and he also had a growing interest in television, the rapidly growing technology finding its way into homes across the United States. He got a job in the television industry, and he quickly realized the power and possibility of this technology and its influence on children—and he wanted to do something positive with it.

This young man came from a family in which he had learned simple and central Christian messages, such as the importance of loving "the Lord your God with all your heart and with all your soul and with all your strength and with all your mind," and, "Love your neighbor as yourself" (Luke 10:27). If you put all those passions, convictions, and interests together, what do you get? You get *Mister Rogers' Neighborhood*, one of the most well-known and beloved children's television programs of the 20th century. Fred Rogers, with his love of music and children and his growing interest and skill in the television industry, along with his belief in the importance of using your gifts to "love your neighbor," touched millions of children's lives with his work.

Fred Rogers' life story is an inspiring example of what happens when you blend educational innovation with deep-seated beliefs, values, and convictions. He did not simply create a television show to be innovative or to make money. He did so as his calling in life.

Frederick Buechner described a calling in this way: "The place God calls you to is the place where your deep gladness and the world's deep hunger meet." It is the place where your unique combination of gifts, talents, abilities, experiences, opportunities, and passions intersect with the needs of the world around you. This might include the people in your home, neighborhood, city, state, region, country, or perhaps throughout the world. The concept of calling recognizes that there is a purpose to who we are and where we find ourselves in the world.

The concept of calling has always been important to me, and I started teaching it to my children when they were very young. I remember one night when my daughter was first learning basic addition. As I discussed the idea of calling and that we have different gifts and abilities that we are called to use in love of our neighbors in the world, I wanted to make it more specific. I wanted my daughter to understand how even the simple facts that she learned in school were related to living out her callings in life. I asked her, "How do you think you can love your brother, one of your neighbors in the world, with math?" I did not have a good answer in my mind, but I thought she might come up with something. I saw her thinking hard about it, but she did not have an answer.

Days later when I came home, my daughter greeted me at the door. I knew as soon as I saw her face that she was excited. "Dad, I did it! I did it!" she exclaimed. "I loved my brother with math!" It turns out that the two of them had been in a dispute earlier in the day about Halloween candy. My wife and I usually take all the candy and put it in a pile to distribute it equally, but that year my daughter and son decided to do it on their own. Naturally, there was a disagreement about what was equal, so my daughter used her newly found math abilities to make sure things were fair and equitable. In her words, she "loved her brother with math." While this might seem like a simple task and example, for her, it came from a place of calling. She used her knowledge and ability to show love to her brother.

For those of us working on educational innovation, I contend that this same line of thinking is an important starting place. Individually, each of us must ask and discover our callings. How does our unique set of gifts, knowledge, abilities, and experiences align with important needs in education? I believe that each person working in the field of education would be wise to grapple with this question until he or she arrives at a compelling answer. That answer will lead them toward a learning organization that values, supports, and desires people with their particular calling.

This question is equally important for an entire learning organization to confront as a whole. Not all learning organizations have the same set of gifts, talents, abilities, experiences, convictions, and passions, nor do they find themselves in the same context or community. Therefore, they do not all have the same callings. Each organization must struggle to understand its unique organizational callings in its given time and place. The more an organization works through this question and comes to collective clarity about it, the more able that organization will be to innovate from a place of purpose, a place that will help it to persist even amid overwhelming challenges and adversity.

Do You Have a Strainer?

Years ago, I became intrigued by highly innovative and outside-the-box learning organizations, and I decided to study such organizations, starting with K-12 schools. I visited, interviewed, observed, and studied publicly available documents about schools that piqued my interest. I wanted to know what was distinct about these schools compared to others, and what these highly innovative schools had in common. After two years of exploration, I found a list of traits common to them all, one of which is especially relevant to this topic of innovating with purpose.

All of these schools had what I now call a strainer. A strainer plays a simple but important role, helping you to identify the important stuff. You pour things into it; those things that fall through the mesh are not important, but what remains in the sifter is the priority. A school's strainer allows people in a school or learning organization to decide what deserves their focus and attention and what does not.

A school strainer consists of one or a few unavoidable, undeniable, school-shaping concepts. These are ideas or core convictions that are nonnegotiable for the school. In the examples I studied, these schools did not have dozens of core convictions. They had only a few, and the people in the school were relentless in sifting new ideas, innovations, and possibilities through these few strainers.

These strainer ideas were specific and everyone had a shared conception of them. An example was a K-12 school that chose to be a project-based learning school, in which students learn through immersive projects rather than teacher-led class sessions. You can easily tell if a school is just dabbling with an idea or if that idea is truly an unavoidable, undeniable school-shaping concept. If project-based learning is indeed one of those strainer ideas, then you will find that every single person in that school is doing work that supports it. You do not see lone ranger teachers closing their doors and doing their own thing counter to project-based learning. That is because a school with a strainer of project-based learning is set up in a way that is almost impossible to resist. They might have even designed the building so that there are no longer doors on classrooms, maybe not even traditional classrooms. Even the architecture supports the core idea.

A strainer idea can be almost anything, but it needs to have certain traits. It needs to be specific and be a part of people's daily thoughts and actions in the school. It guides each decision and allows a school to decide what not to do as much as what to do. People sift programs, projects, ideas, policies, and practices through that strainer. Further, it protects learning organizations from chasing shiny things, pursuing the latest educational innovation just because it is new and trendy. It gives the school a distinct identity that can easily be recognized by even a first-time visitor, and the school becomes known for this idea. Finally, there is a tough-minded approach of no exceptions. People do not compromise on it. You might hear some defend it by simply saying something like, "This is who we are," or, "If they don't like it, then maybe this isn't the right place for them." That last quote might seem harsh, but it speaks to the shared ownership, buy-in, and conviction that inform their attachment to an unavoidable, undeniable, school-shaping concept.

School-shaping concepts come in myriad forms. A school might have a methodology based on any one of such various philosophies as project-based learning, inquiry-based learning, self-directed learning, or service learning, or it might have a conviction about how it serves learners. For example, imagine a school that made "no child left behind" its school-shaping concept and further imagine that everyone in the organization agreed upon what that phrase meant. I am not referring to the federal program with similar appellation here but to a core conviction about how that school would serve every student, absolutely refusing to let any single learner be left behind in learning opportunities. Imagine the power and possibilities that would come from an organization that made this core conviction a daily mantra, something that shaped every hiring decision, influenced every new program or possibility, directed every budgeting decision, and framed every innovation. Such a school would be a truly distinctive one, with a compelling vision that informed when and how it pursued educational innovation.

What Is Your "Every Day" Statement?

I was in a coffee shop meeting with a colleague when I saw a young woman standing in line to give her order. I was struck by the words printed on the back of her t-shirt, a shirt worn by Walgreens employees at that time. It said, "Every day I help people get, stay, and live well." That slogan became a reminder for me about the importance of learning organizations and the people in them having what I now call an "every day statement."

An every day statement is something that an organization is committed to doing every single day with no exceptions. It is a way of representing the heart of an organization's mission and convictions. What is so central to what that organization does that it happens every day? Whatever the statement is, it should not be mundane or transactional but should be crafted with inspirational and substantive language.

One way for a learning organization to stay grounded is for the organization itself and every person in that organization to have an every day statement. On the organizational level, it might be something like, "Every day we help people develop knowledge and skill that equips them to live good, meaningful, and powerful lives." It should be a sentence or a phrase around which people can rally, something that they are proud to wake up to each day. And at the end of the day, they can fall asleep thankful for being part of an organization with such an every day statement.

Each person in a learning organization can also have his or her own every day statement. The person working in the front office might have a different every day statement from that of a classroom teacher or professor. A building administrator might have a different one from a person who provides special services or support in another way. The important part is that each person frames what he or she is doing around a statement of mission and effectiveness.

Organizations that have such statements to influence and inspire people are more likely to innovate from a place of meaning and substance. The innovations they undertake, then, aren't merely about doing something new and trendy, but they have a real and tangible effect on people's lives. That is the type of innovation that we want to pursue, and we want people in the organization having strong thoughts and feelings about what is done because they believe so deeply in their individual missions as well as in the organizational mission.

What Is Your Compelling Reason?

Simon Sinek's TED talk about his concept "the golden circle" and his subsequent book *Start with Why* was about a secret that many great organizations share. Sinek pointed out that the best organizations have, at their centers, a compelling reason, and that is where they start. In other words, at the heart of the organization, they talk about why they exist. After that, they attend to how they do it, and third, they look at what they do. Not only that, but the part about why they exist is not just a one-time exercise that results in a document that collects dust in someone's office. It is a part of their culture and daily conversation.

Sinek's circle is as effective for schools and learning organizations as it is for businesses. As I've looked at innovative learning organizations that have a measurable effect, I've noticed that they all know why they exist, and they are quick to talk about that compelling reason with one another and with visitors. Their compelling reason drives their conversation about how and what they will do. The reason a learning organization exists will shape that organization's core beliefs and philosophy about education, topics that are essential to missional innovation.

When I was in graduate school years ago, one of my professors told the story of a doctoral student who chose to study the reasons why students fall asleep in class, using a qualitative research method known as grounded theory. In that method, you start with a core research question and then conduct in-depth interviews with the population of people who are most likely to help you answer that research question.

The researcher interviewed students who fell asleep in at least one class during the past semester. As he conducted the interviews, he began to develop a theory that provided an answer to his core research question. Then he interviewed more people, seeing if data from those subsequent interviews supported or deviated from his existing theory. He adjusted his theory to accommodate the data from each new interview, continuing this process until he had a theory that adequately explained the data gathered from all of the interviewees.

Finally, the researcher distilled his theory about why students fall asleep in class down to a simple two-word phrase, "perceived meaninglessness." In other words, the reason students fell asleep in class had nothing to do with how the students felt, how much they had slept the night before, or any other such physical explanation. When learners perceive that what is happening in a class lacks meaning, they lose motivation and are more likely to fall asleep.

If that is the case for individual learners, how much more is it true for learning organizations? To state it bluntly, perceived meaninglessness can put an entire organization to sleep. However, when an organization has a meaningful, well understood, and compelling reason why the organization exists, that organization is far more likely to be inspired and to be pursuing innovations that make a difference in people's lives.

Over the past decade, as my writing has gained attention, I started to get more consulting and speaking requests than I could accept, and I had to find a way to prioritize these requests. So, when someone reached out to me, I responded first by asking that person to share a single goal that they wanted to accomplish through my speaking or consulting for them. Many of them wanted help in informing a group about the possibilities for digital-age teaching and learning, moving toward a given educational innovation, or preparing for the future of education.

Others were not sure, and they wanted me to suggest some ideas for them. To better understand whether what I had to offer might be a good fit with those organizations, I worked my way through one or more of the following questions:

- Why does your organization exist?
- What is your organization's mission and how well do people know and support this mission?
- What is distinct about your organization, or what do you want to be distinct about it?
- What kind difference do you want to make in the world through your organization?
- What are the core values, beliefs, or convictions that shape what your organization does right now?

When there was a specific innovation in mind, the most important question I asked is, "Why?" Why do you want to pursue this innovation? Why is this innovation important to you and those whom you serve? Why do you think this innovation is important to your organizational mission, vision, values, and goals? Their answers to these questions usually determined whether I was willing to work with them or how I would proceed. I was looking for a compelling reason. If there was no compelling reason, I would either decline to consult or speak for them, or I would suggest that my work with them begin with helping them to develop a compelling reason for their organization's existence.

In fact, when I work with a client to help cultivate shared ownership, I either invite participants to communicate the reason behind their organization, or I offer a case for a compelling reason. People do follow ideas that don't have a compelling reason behind them, but those ideas are generally the fashionable and trend-based innovations in education, wasting time and precious resources. Those are ideas that may spread easily, but they are missional dead ends, and they will either change or stifle an organization's mission.

This is why it is important to be informed about the trends and innovations, but to consistently and persistently discuss them only in light of your organization's reason for being. Highly effective, mission-minded organizations have little room for compromise. If people in the organization do not buy into the fundamental reason behind the organization, then the organization has a mission-critical situation. There is a leak in the ship, and if the leak is a big one, the entire mission is in danger of sinking.

My challenge to myself these days is to awaken in myself, in the organizations that I serve, and in others a deeper sense of the reasons behind the educational innovations that I support. In fact, this personal challenge is what sets my work and writing apart. If you scan my books, articles, and blog posts, you will find that I consistently weave an exploration of the reasons behind the trends that I report on. Rarely will I merely write a how-to article about problem-based learning, the flipped classroom, game-based learning, educational leadership, self-directed learning, blended learning, online learning, or any other educational innovation without also delving into the reasons behind those innovations.

I explore plenty of practical steps and review numerous emerging innovations, but I strive to do so in a way that grapples with foundational questions about why those innovations matter. Without a fundamental understanding of who we are and why we do the things we do, we are, in the words of William Ralph Inge, destined "marry the spirit of the age, only to find ourselves widows and widowers tomorrow." Instead, let us marry the mission and use only those trends that strengthen the marriage. Let us innovate with intent, with purpose, and from a place of deep conviction. Let us be champions for innovations that truly serve mission-driven education.

2

Educational Innovation and Global Change

Sixty-six years. That is the time between the Wright Brothers' first flight and the 1969 Apollo 11 landing on the moon. In 2015, as I write this essay, I note that it has coincidentally been 66 years since the invention of the airsickness bags that sit in the pocket in front of you on the plane. While there have been subtle changes to the latter innovation, those changes pale in comparison to the rapid evolution from first flight to landing on the moon.

Why is it that innovation skyrockets in some areas but develops gradually in others?

Innovations Soar when They Capture the Imagination

The imagination is a powerful catalyst for innovation, and the idea of flight compelled people to imagine and dream, creating enough excitement to generate completely new fields of study. On the other hand, airsickness bags address a real need, but can anyone really get excited about the next innovation for capturing the result of mid-air emesis?

Does It Inspire an Adventure or Merely Meet a Need?

Of course we need simple and practical innovations that address heretofore unmet needs, but the innovations that thrill us are the ones that awaken our thirst for adventure and discovery and allow us to join our Star Trek friends as we, "boldly go where no one has gone before."

A Compelling Vision Will Inspire a Broad Community of Innovators

When the Wright brothers took flight, they fulfilled a centuries-long dream, and that dream's fulfillment led to even grander dreams. Before long, a diverse community of innovators began to contribute other, smaller innovations, from communications technologies to rocket science, that eventually culminated in a landing on the moon.

Call Out the Vision that Leads the Way

While both of the two innovations mentioned earlier—airplanes and airsickness bags—arose from the vision of flight, only one inspires, while the other addresses one of the practical challenges that occurred as humans became accustomed to vehicular flight. Who needs an airsickness bag if you can't fly? And yet, considering the broader problem of motion sickness, humanity has gained much from the growth of scientific knowledge around emesis since the invention of the first airsickness bag. The dream of flight led the way, but multiple more humble innovations followed in the wake of flight itself.

In your work as an educational innovator, look for the vision that most inspires, the one that encompasses the not-so-lofty ones.

Applying These Lessons

Now let's apply these simple lessons to educational innovation:

Lead with a Grand Dream

Before you start investing in countless gadgets, technologies, or new models for education, clarify your dream. Is it big? It is worthy of your life's work? Is it clear and compelling? Is it capable of rallying a group of diverse people to accomplish it? If so, get to work. You might be the one to lay the groundwork of exploring the possibilities, or you might be one who helps make one or more of the possibilities a reality. Either way, use what you have to contribute to the dream.

Focus on the Larger Goal

It is easy for us to invest the bulk of our energy working on the educational equivalent of airsickness bags, small innovations that make educational life a little more convenient or bearable. In fact, it is possible to spend an entire lifetime on such trivialities without realizing it.

Be one of those who are willing to dream grand visions of what could be possible in education, ignoring the naysayers, gaining inspiration from the possibilities and the nobility of the vision, and persistently driving toward your goal. As one of those grand dreamers, you will likely need numerous micro-innovations along your way. Embrace them and learn about them, but keep putting them into the context of the grand goal. As Mark Twain once wrote, "You can't depend on your eyes when your imagination is out of focus."

Invite Others to Join You

Neil Armstrong didn't get to the moon on his own. The flight at Kitty Hawk represented an important step in that direction, and countless other courageous individuals carried the dream through the 66 years between the two flights. Find inspiration, support, and encouragement from a growing group of other people who share your vision. Many of the grandest innovations in history arose from cooperative communities working together, and the same is true for the boldest visions for education today. A small community forms around a shared vision that often grows as it gains momentum.

Embrace Your Place

It is hard for any one of us to know what role we play inside the dream of a truly grand vision. Some will be like Da Vinci, sketching out possibilities hundreds of years before they happen. Someone else will be one of a pair of brothers, building early prototypes that inspire a generation of others to take that work to a level that is unimaginable to those brothers. Maybe you are the one who will design that first rocket, or you may be a member of the support crew for the first launch, or maybe you'll even be the lucky one to get to set foot on the moon. You won't know in the beginning which part you'll play. Embrace the dream, then commit to the goal, identify and use your gifts in the pursuit of it, and enjoy your unique role. One day you will sit back and take pride in whatever ways—whether small or central—you helped to make that vision a reality.

3

Be Yourself and More of Yourself

What does a school, university, or learning organization need to do to grow and thrive in the future of education? Follow my writing online and elsewhere and you will read a dozen answers to that question, but here is one perspective that you haven't heard from me before: We need learning organizations that are "all in" on being themselves, the best and most distinct version of that self. That is not to say that an organization should ignore all promising trends and emerging practices. There are times to embrace and assimilate new practices, but there are also times to kindly pass on a trend because it is not right for your organization.

I realize that some people will misread the preceding paragraph, thinking of it as an invitation for the Sweet Briar colleges of the world to refuse any changes that might give them a fighting chance to survive and even thrive, but that isn't what I mean. I am referring to innovating from a deep and authentic organizational identity.

In my consulting, visiting, and learning from different organizations, it has become easier for me to recognize when an organization knows itself. A person who knows himself or herself tends to have an interesting blend of rigidity along with a willingness to explore new possibilities with a delightful dispassionate curiosity. Such a person can experiment and explore new options while staying grounded in who they are, retaining their core values and identity. While such methods might baffle some and frustrate others, they make sense to that person and he or she stays the course. So it is with an organization that knows itself and holds to its values.

Those organizations that do not have a strong sense of their collective identity are the ones that either blow in the wind or stand firm, fists clenched, like a stubborn child standing between a tornado and his beloved sandbox. The wind blowers float from one trend to another, hoping they can stay in the air longer than others or maybe soar above the rest. The stubborn children, on the other hand, cling to traditions, practices, and policies with religious fervor, ready to close their doors for good instead of making the slightest adjustments. They remain unchanged, striving to convince themselves and others about how all the changes around them are overstated, over-rated, and unworthy of serious attention or consideration. "Ah. That isn't a tornado! That is just a strong wind," they'll say. Often enough, they throw some strong moral language, righteous anger, or intellectual disgust into their statements, just enough to add some extra resolve and derogate the other. I've been both the wind blower and the stubborn child at various times, but I nonetheless hold up this ideal of the organization that knows itself even as it moves into the future.

I'm drawn to organizations that have distinct flavors. By that I mean I'm drawn to organizations that have a strategy of building on their own distinctions. This strategy is not about resisting change. It is about being who they are as an organization and building on that, becoming even more of that self. It is about knowing the innovations that amplify, clarify, and extend their core identity and values. What this means and looks like will vary by organization, but distinct organizations that know themselves have a way of drawing a following of people who value that identity and share the same values.

4

Being a Humble Educational Radical

radical[rad-i-kuh l] – thoroughgoing or extreme, especially as regards change from accepted or traditional forms. – *http://dictionary.reference.com/browse/radical*

Perhaps some of my ideas about education are radical, but I like to think that I strive to at least be a humble sort of radical. By that I mean I hardly ever advocate that one of my ideas should become the standard by which all other ideas and proposals must be measured. I rarely argue that they should be national policy, and I don't contend that my concepts should be universal. In fact, one of the few broad concepts that I consistently do advocate for is a diversity of ideas, practices, models, and frameworks in education. In other words, if I had to advocate for a policy that would direct all of education, it would be for a policy that promoted variety and choice, recognizing that one model or framework is not best for all learners in all places and at all times. Therefore, I spend more of my time exploring education reform by design and not by policy, even though I have a persistent and growing interest in policy as design.

Education policy is simply the phrase used to describe the many laws and rules that govern and direct education in different domains. Some extend this definition to include laws and policies—for example, economic policies—that are not explicitly about education but which affect education systems. These policies have immense influence in our K-12 and higher education organizations.

Rules that affect education are established at all levels, beginning with schools themselves and extending to the national level. People establish policies with the goal of shaping the education system, protecting certain stakeholders, amplifying certain values and goals, and embodying a given philosophy of education. It works. Policies do change schools and perspectives on education, sometimes in seemingly positive ways. Other times these policies produce incredibly destructive results.

Quite often, the philosophies, values, and motives behind new or longstanding policies are unclear. Sometimes that is by design. Sometimes it is lost in the sound bites. Other times such foundations are forgotten or ignored for one reason or another. Regardless, I take policy seriously. Policymakers are establishing laws and rules that affect other people's lives and education. They are restricting people from more freely embracing certain beliefs and convictions about education while empowering other beliefs and convictions.

A policy produces losers and winners. It is never neutral. It always elevates some people and not others, and when the advocates of a new policy champion it as the best for the community or a larger population, they are often espousing a personal philosophy that they claim will be best for all or most.

Change the Rules to Win the Game

From an early age, my son really liked winning games. From that perspective, he also discovered that one of the more effective ways to win at a game is through policymaking. Just change the rules or lobby to change the rules, he realized, so that the game favors your preferences and strengths and disregards your limitations. Such lobbying is an obvious ploy by a five-year-old boy, but what about when a fifty-year-old policymaker does the same? Or, what about when the arguments are shaped by the voices and influence of dozens or hundreds of different stakeholders, each wanting to win or gain something? Some of those stakeholders might frame their gain as a noble cause, the very thing that is best for society. Others might be willing to be flexible about how they want to lobby for the benefits of a very specific population.

As much as I don't like to think of education as a game with rules, the metaphor holds up quite well when we look at the positioning of various people and groups and their lobbying for different regulations. The U.S. Department of Education, for example, often seems to protect the government's investment in financial aid for higher education, quickly followed by issues related to workforce development and gainful employment. Other governmental agencies appear to have layers of priorities. Even as they argue that they are champions of innovation, their policies represent a fervent effort to slow innovation and protect traditional concepts of the teacher, the professorate, the diploma, the college degree, and dozens of other priorities in K-12 or higher education.

Yet, the closer you get to this world, the more convoluted things get. There are unquestionably multiple layers of motive. There are even those who appear to think of a single policy change as if it were a chess move intended to set themselves up for success five or six moves in the future. What these people seem to have forgotten is that people's lives are affected by every policy change.

Since this is the context in which we live and work as we walk toward growth and improvement in education, humility and choice are vitally important. With such powerfully competing interests, we can't afford a monopolized approach to educational policy. It doesn't matter how honorable or trustworthy the leadership is at a given time and at a given level. We may not be able to do much about policy monopolies at individual learning organizations, but beyond that hyperlocal level, we can build a system that empowers choice, nurtures innovation and creativity, rejects a one-size-fits-all approach, and most importantly recognizes the tentative nature of our knowledge about what does and does not work at different times, places, and contexts in education. At the same time, we must be careful to retain reasonable levels of accountability while doing away with massive hindrances, and we must keep in mind that others will have different goals and philosophies that need to be taken into account.

Butterflies and Tsunamis

Could it be that a butterfly flapping its wings on one side of the world might cause a tsunami on the other side of the world? This is a classic question in chaos theory, but it is also something that I think about with the often difficult-to-predict implications of making even the smallest policy changes. Could it be that an educational policy flapping its wings at the federal or national level might cause an educational tsunami in a local school? We might have good intentions, but there are so many complexities and factors that we are often unaware of the full effect of our policies. I'm not arguing that we refrain from any policy, but realizing that we cannot know all of the implications calls us to be sober and thoughtful before lobbying for our ideas to become the gold standard in education.

For those of us who might verge on being radical in education, the same is true. Let us pursue our efforts with passion tempered with humility. Instead of forcing our ideas and opinions on the largest possible population through rules and regulations, let the effects of our work speak for themselves.

5

Traits of Innovative Schools and Their Leaders

For about three years, I visited numerous schools in the kindergarten through high school range that were receiving significant attention for being innovative. The schools varied significantly: from urban to rural, large to small, elementary to secondary, private to public, start-ups to well established schools, and with varying levels of diversity. Some of those schools had a track record of strong student gains and achievement; others had not been around long enough to provide such data.

For the sake of my explorations, I kept a broad definition of "innovative," leaning more toward schools that considered themselves to be innovative and had a community of external stakeholders who agreed. Generally, they were schools that saw themselves as ahead of the times, breaking the mold of traditional schooling.

I continue to visit more schools each year, and I am beginning to develop a list of traits that are consistent among the schools I have visited so far. Ten traits emerge among the leaders and others in these highly innovative schools. I offer these ten traits as a guide for other schools that aspire to increase their capacity for missional innovation.

Visionary Leadership, but not Necessarily Earth-Shattering Inventions

Some of the leaders I visited, interviewed, and learned from were truly world-class in their knowledge and expertise. Others were not. They were all intelligent and informed, but some were just good at drawing together the best ideas from other organizations and putting them together in an innovative way. However, every one of these leaders could communicate the vision for the school brilliantly. They had a clear vision, and they talked about it with clarity and conviction. If they had to give an elevator speech about that vision, they would hit it out of the park, every time.

One or Two Clear, Unavoidable, School-Shaping Concepts

I mentioned this factor in an earlier chapter. These highly innovative organizations did not overwhelm themselves with a long list of distinguishing traits that were central to their organizational mission and identity. They focused on one or a few of them. However, for those few concepts, these leaders were relentless and unswerving. These were truly school-shaping concepts, not just ideas embraced by one unit or a small group of forward-thinking leaders. These were differentiating traits, and everyone in the organization was expected to value and champion these concepts.

Tough Mindset from Principals and Teachers

The leaders in these schools represented many personalities and leadership styles. Some were extroverts. Others were introverts. Some were pastoral while others were more authoritarian. Some were quick to speak about their achievement and successes while others did not seem comfortable talking about what they did well. Regardless of these differences, all of the leaders in these highly innovative organizations were incredibly bold and assertive when it came down the school-shaping concepts. There was no room for compromise. There was no room for teachers or others who challenged or disagreed with those core concepts. When it came to these core ideas, these leaders were tough and unswerving, and their decisions reflected that. They might not have enjoyed it, but they were willing to hire and fire on the basis of these ideals. They were also not going to let any practice or policy into the building that undermined these ideals.

Extensive Research Before Implementation

These were not just leaders who had a good idea and started a school on a whim. It was not just a good idea acquired at a conference. They did their homework. Then they did some more. Some conducted formal research. All of them did some form of extensive research before they stepped into leadership or started the organization. They visited other schools, read widely, thought deeply, or learned from mentors. From this research, they built a confidence, along with depth, expertise, clarity of vision, and conviction about the worthiness of the cause. Quite often, they began to build a team or community around the cause because of their research.

Even after implementation, the research continued. These leaders did not just rely on the first set of ideas that they helped implement. They continued to research, to learn new possibilities, and to consider how these new ideas might support the core convictions of the school.

Once the Vision Was Clear, Strong Alliance with Like-Minded Organizations

Many school leaders connect and collaborate with other schools nearby. In other words, their alliance is based on proximity as much or more than on shared vision. This is not the case with the leaders of these highly innovative organizations. They established alliances with other like-minded leaders and organizations, even if those other organizations were in another part of the world. In some cases, the leaders established their own network to build alliances with like-minded people and to help expand the vision to other parts of the country or world. In other instances, they found existing organizations and leaders who closely aligned with their core convictions. Either way, they formed alliances they valued, but those alliances had to be ones that strengthened the mission and helped them make progress.

Near Addiction to Effectiveness and Impact Data—and Obvious Use of that Data, Especially Related to Student Learning

These leaders were on a mission. It was not just about looking innovative or being perceived as successful. They had goals, priorities, and convictions. They wanted to know that they were achieving their goals, that their priorities were protected, and that their convictions were honored. They craved feedback in various forms. Some were highly analytical and loved crunching numbers about effectiveness. Others relied more heavily on qualitative feedback from diverse sources. They wanted feedback from visitors, learners, teachers, parents, and anyone else who might provide a helpful perspective. Then they used this feedback to adjust and improve what they were doing.

This means that they did not just want people to compliment them. They wanted to skip through the niceties and get at something that would help them get better. This was not about ego. It was about the pursuit of excellence, and these leaders understood that candid and thoughtful feedback was essential.

Unusually High Turnover

As I've visited more mature organizations, this trait is less evident, but it was especially true in organizations that were part of an established system. For such organizations, there was no small amount of turnover when it came to finding the right teachers. First, these schools were distinct, sometimes unique, so it could be hard to find people who were the right fit for that organization or who were open to making the change in personal practices and convictions to support such a school. Regardless, with these innovative schools, people quickly learned if they were not a good fit, and often chose to leave. When they didn't, leadership would step in and invite them to explore new possibilities in a different job.

Highly Protective of What (or Who) They Put in the Water

What is important about unusually high turnover and this trait is that the leaders were unrelenting in their adherence to the school-shaping concepts. The school is not shaped or reshaped by individual preferences. It is a truly mission-driven organization that is not willing to let personnel compromise that.

The flip side of this attribute is that the people who fit in the organization really fit. They spoke about their work at the school as life-changing or as a dream come true. The people who stayed were all in on the mission and core convictions. They became just as mission-minded and unswerving as the founders and leaders.

Significant Investment in Ongoing Professional Development, Especially Investing in New People

Because there are often no existing pathways or training programs to prepare people for work in these innovative and distinct organizations, the organizations had to do one of several things. Some created their own training, sometimes making it a perquisite to work at the school. Some hired people who had experience in similar organizations. Others looked for people with the right set of convictions and basic skills, and then invested in their growth and development along the way. Whatever the case, if they wanted their core convictions to be lived out in these people, the leaders realized that this meant an investment in ongoing professional development.

These organizations didn't just have random workshops or guest presenters. The professional development was owned by the people who worked there, but there was rich sharing and collaboration among them. For most of these organizations, they had established a true and robust learning community among the staff, often revolving around current projects and priorities in the school.

Learning was an institutional priority and lifestyle in these organizations. Some of these schools used all or part of "summer break" for staff learning, retooling, and collaboration. Some would invest immense money sending people to specialized training at some of the top organizations in the world. What was clear was that they didn't just do professional development to meet some licensure requirement or to check a box for promotion. It was central to their calling and career, meaningful and substantive.

Committed to Sharing Their Secret with Others

As these organizations mature and gain a reputation for their success and distinctiveness, there is often an opportunity to share what they are doing with the world. I have yet to meet a leader of such an organization who does not eventually get to this stage. Some speak, write, and mentor. Others establish networks to help launch similar schools. Regardless, when you experience something this transformational and personally meaningful, it is hard to keep it a secret. Like the well-known TED Talks, people in these schools develop "ideas worth sharing."

6

Disposable Rafts: Fail Fast and Reflect Often

A man traveling along the banks of a river found himself in a dangerous place. He noticed what appeared to be a safe place on the other side of the river, but the water in the river was high and swirling fast and there was no boat or bridge in sight. He gathered sticks and twigs, and with them he built a simple raft that carried him safely across to the other side, where he continued his journey on dry land. What do you suppose he did with the raft when he got to the other side? Of course, he left it behind, as it had served its purpose and he had no further use for it.

The Buddha's raft parable is one of the better-known stories of Buddhism, told in many ways and simply stated in the Diamond Sutra. "Understand that the words of the Buddha are like a raft built to cross a river: When its purpose is completed, it must be left behind if we are to travel further!"

While the lessons of this parable are intended to instruct followers about the nature of the dharma or the teachings of the Buddha, I sometimes think about this parable in terms of educational trends and innovations. How are trends like rafts and when is it time to leave them behind? Trends have their time and place, but they are never the mission.

I've met many educators, parents, and administrators who critique the nearly constant trends and innovations that flow like a river into educational circles for a while and then just as quickly flow past. There is truth and value in these critiques because without them we risk becoming drawn to the next shiny thing little consideration about a particular innovation's benefits and limitations. We need to examine the data and research, and we need to analyze the trends in light of how well they serve the greater purpose and mission of a particular learning organization.

At the same time, the Buddha's raft parable gives us another useful perspective on the role of educational trends and innovations. I find it helpful to see these trends and innovations as tools that can help us to deal with our current challenges and opportunities. They are like disposable rafts that we use and then leave behind, for isn't it true that you only need a raft as long as you need to cross a river? Once you are on dry land again, there is little need for such a vessel. At that point, you likely need an altogether different set of resources.

When it comes to thinking about educational trends, innovations, and technologies, our needs for them depend upon the context, the learner profile, the current challenges, and the prevailing opportunities. As new knowledge and technologies develop, we find tools that better meet our needs than did those of the past. This is the nature of tools. While we need to avoid mindless meandering from one trend to the next, perhaps it is helpful to see these fast-moving trends as useful devices, albeit temporary and transient ones.

The raft parable also prompts me to look at perceived failures with educational trends and innovations from another angle. Yes, some efforts and innovations are largely and widely seen as failures, sometimes because they did not live up the promises attached to them. Others failed because of lack of planning and a limited consideration for the scope of the project.

When an innovative project is unsuccessful, some abandon their efforts toward innovation, label the experience a failure, and move on. It just didn't work out, they'll say. Still others look at it more strategically. What did we learn from this effort that we might not otherwise have discovered about ourselves, about the learners, about the need for planning and research, and about the importance of involving different stakeholders? Without such "failures," certain important lessons might remain hidden from us, and, further, it might be difficult for anyone to pass these lessons on to others. There are so many lessons to gain from a failed effort, if we are open to embracing those experiences as learning opportunities.

This line of thinking is not intended as a defense of poor planning, careless experimentation, or casual indifference toward stewardship of time and resources. There is wisdom in conducting small experiments before trying larger ones, taking the time to review the research, and going through a systematic process. Yet, even the best plans do not always produce the best results. So, we learn to fail fast, reflect often, and extract as much meaning and learning as possible from our efforts. And as the goals, contexts, and technological landscape change, we will likely still find ourselves leaving even our favorite rafts behind as we continue our learning journey.

I have left a lot of rafts behind in my travels through educational innovation and experimentation, many of which I once regarded as embarrassments and failures. Yet, from my perspective now, I also see how work on some of these "failures" led to some of my recent successes. Perhaps those experiences we think of as failures are not always failures after all. Maybe they were just disposable rafts that served their purpose for a time and made future adventures possible.

7

Individual Preference Versus Collective Practice

What reigns in your learning organization: individual preferences or collective practices?

There is a persistent tension in learning organizations when it comes to deciding how to do things. Some argue for a culture that gives immense freedom for individual preferences to reign supreme. Others argue for more consistency throughout the organization and uniform practice, calling for individuals to set aside some of their personal preferences for that which is determined to better serve the mission, the learners, or the organization as a whole. Still others strive to find a reasonable balance between the two. Regardless, I've come to suspect that so much conflict in learning organizations, especially secondary and tertiary institutions, seems connected to this tension. I've also begun to notice that how an organization deals with this tension says a great deal about its health and identity.

More than twenty years ago, as a new student in a graduate program, I went to sign up for my second quarter of classes. I was a night owl at the time, enjoying hours each night reading, writing, and thinking. While I enjoyed classes, I enjoyed even more the freedom and free-flowing thinking in those late-night hours, when I would often explore a provocative question or idea through half the night. That was my favorite part of the day, even as I valued traditional classes along with countless rich and rewarding informal conversations with classmates.

So, when I went into that large room on that day to meet with my advisors and sign up for my next quarter of classes, I was troubled when I learned that a class I needed was available only at seven in the morning three days a week. At that stage in my life, that seemed like an intolerable option. It would destroy my beloved late nights, when I could get lost in books and ideas until two or three in the morning. In fact, I decided that it was too much of a sacrifice, and I dropped out of the graduate program that day, in some ways changing the entire trajectory of my life's work. For some people who knew me then, that seems like an absurd decision. If only I had been willing to submit to the systems and processes of the institution, imagine how much more I could have benefited. Yet for me, at that point in my life, I was unwilling to give up my individual approach to learning for the sake of institutional processes.

This memory highlights the tension experienced by both teachers and learners in many learning organizations. Each one has his or her own individual preferences, personal habits, and values, and each also has goals that involve benefiting from what the learning organization has to offer. Then, too, the organization also has its values, practices, rituals, and expectations. Some people find it possible to achieve a balance between the two. Others submit to organizational preferences, or even to the whims of individual professors, even when those whims seem unreasonable or an unnecessary nuisance. Those people learn to put up with others' expectations, keep their heads down, and make it through the program.

What About the Educators?

Individual teachers usually prefer doing something one way over another. Some have come to these preferences through careful thought, study, analysis, refinement over years of experience, or maybe even through more calculated experimentation. Others are just going with their past experience, comfort, intuition, or some other internal guidance. Sometimes they are well aware that these are just their preferences. Other times educators burn these preferences into their fundamental belief systems and philosophies about education, so much so that they are willing to take their final stand on an individual versus collective tension. Such a stand seems, in the big picture, as strange to me now as does my dropping out of a graduate program because I had to take an early-morning class.

Educators' preferences might have to do with class schedules, classroom procedures, grading methods, assessment and feedback plans, teaching methods, classroom management practices, communication styles, and other plans and procedures. From this perspective, teaching is an art, and people might argue that you don't want to stifle an artist by imposing your rules or expectations on them. Just as often, it is ultimately just about the individual teachers wanting the autonomy to do things how they want to do them. And for many teachers, the idea of accountability, in most forms, is an attack on one's professional prerogative.

Limited Flexibility

Then there is the other side, the learning organization that gives very little freedom or flexibility to the individual. Everything is spelled out, dictated, and directed. You do it the organization's way or you find a different place to work or learn. It is the same mindset that you might see among some teachers in how they manage the classroom, or in the words of some teachers, "their" classroom. Those teachers see the classroom as the teacher's domain and the teacher as the benevolent, albeit academically rigorous, dictator.

Top Organizations Work Through this Dilemma

As I've learned from visiting countless learning organizations, the best ones have found a way through this tension. They have at least a small set of unavoidable, undeniable school-shaping concepts that are truly nonnegotiable, and those concepts drive common practices. The people in that organization have bought into the distinct mission and vision of the organization enough so that they are willing to set aside some of their personal preferences for the collective ones. At the same time, when a practice isn't integral to the core school-shaping concepts, the organization leaves room for individual preferences and practices.

The organizations that struggle the most with this tension are the ones experiencing an identity crisis. They have less of a shared mission, vision, values, and goals. Because of this lack of a common vision, there is mistrust, a weak culture, and/or persistent disagreement about what really matters for all people and what should be left to individual preferences. There is no functional forum in which the community can work through these differences, come to an agreement about a shared mission, and discuss their differences in view of their shared mission, vision, values, and goals. "Everyone [does] what is right in their own eyes," and there is no longer a distinct culture. In the end, what might have been a community is now just a collection of people.

Proverbs 29 reminds us that, "When there is no vision, the people perish," and this quote seems to me to represent a truth in learning organizations as well.

I am becoming increasingly confident that a key to the success of educational institutions and communities in the emerging landscape comes down to identifying undeniable, unavoidable school-shaping distinctives that resonate with and provide significant value to a target population.

For the innovative learning organization, this is even more important. Countless innovations and experiments that are not tied to a central or shared vision will quickly destroy the culture, exhaust individuals, and leave the community uncertain about the ultimate goals or purpose of that community.

There will always be tension between individual preferences or ways of doing things and those that are institution-wide. While such tensions will destroy the visionless organization, the very same tensions may well strengthen the organization that lifts up and revolves around a set of well understood, highly regarded core concepts or operating principles.

8

Three Conditions for Successful School Innovation

In *Seeing What's Next: Using Theories of Innovation to Predict Industry Change*, Clayton M. Christensen, Erik A. Roth, and Scott D. Anthony describe one of the reasons many organizations don't adapt to or embrace disruptive innovation. They point to the resources, processes, and values (RPV) theory for their explanation.

Resources are the human and other resources that exist in a given organization. Processes are the way the organization functions, its systems and policies, and the processes that shape the way things get done. Values are the organizational priorities, those things an organizational culture values or wants to accomplish.

These three elements help us to understand the strengths of an organization as well as to see what the organization fails to recognize, those areas the authors refer to as "blind spots." Of the three elements, an organization's resources tend to be the most flexible, while the other two resist change and tend to persist. When an organization has the necessary resources, along with a set of values that helps them to prioritize effectively and processes that aid in them in reaching their core goals, they usually have a recipe for success.

What happens when an opportunity arises that does not align with the organizational processes, values, and resources? In many cases, the organization passes on the opportunity. Maybe a few people in the organization see the opportunity and try to pursue it, but their efforts likely end in frustration. Even if those perceptive innovators have the necessary resources, the project is likely to fail, especially if they must try to work within the organization's existing policies. In other scenarios favorable policies and values exist, but there are inadequate resources. One of the best ways to ensure a failed attempt at implementing an innovation in a learning organization is to try to force it into the existing processes and provide it with fewer resources than it needs. Consider the following examples.

The One-to-One Program

Let's say that a principal or university dean sees that other schools are moving to one-to-one programs. This dean or principal decides that she needs to keep up with those other schools by implementing a similar initiative. However, the faculty in her school value specific teaching strategies that don't require a one-to-one program. Furthermore, those teachers have a history of allowing new technologies into their classrooms, but only when they can just use those technologies to substitute for previous technologies. For a couple of examples, they are fine with a SMART Board® because they largely use it like a white board; and the professor or teacher who loves to lecture is fine with using PowerPoint because it replaces the old overhead projector slides.

To make matters worse, many of the policies and processes within the school, and especially within specific classes, seek to manage student behavior by means of rigid methods of classroom management. Finally, the leader wants to implement her move to one-to-one programs without investing too much money in the infrastructure that would be necessary for successful one-to-one learning, such as increased Internet bandwidth, professional development for faculty, and the time and money it would take to cultivate shared ownership among key stakeholders. Perhaps some resources are available, but they are limited, and given the existing processes and teachers' values, the leader's half-hearted initiative has little chance of success.

Online Programs at a University

In another example, one or more university leaders have a vision for reaching new students by adding online programs. Most faculty at the school view online learning with suspicion, so there are few volunteers to help out. In addition, the project leaders who want to add online programs try to use the same marketing, recruitment, and admissions processes that are used for the rest of the university. They also expect existing student support systems to function as well for online students as they do for more traditional students.

Before the project gets very far along at all, the project leaders find that enrollments are down, the academic quality is questionable, and student satisfaction is low because students have trouble navigating the internal offices and finding people who understand and appreciate the unique challenges of an online learner. For instance, it doesn't work well for someone studying from a thousand miles away to hear, "Just stop by the office and we can work this out."

The School Within a School

A traditional high school decides to launch a new innovative school within a school, one that focuses upon a particular area or method, as a charter or magnet school might do. It might be that the school within a school is planned as a STEM academy or a school of the arts, or maybe it would be focused around project-based learning, self-directed learning, service learning, or experiential education.

However, the school board and the school leadership decide that this new school must work within the existing processes of the original school. They must use the same grading system, the same daily schedule, and so on. In addition, the high school decides to implement this new school within a school on a shoestring budget, providing no discretionary funds and no dedicated space.

Not even the most talented and dynamic leader would be likely to achieve success given all these handicaps. Unless at some point, resources, processes, and values are put in place to support it, the program is bound to fail. What is likely to happen instead is that the initiative will become a good course or supplemental program within the school, a variation of the core school experience, but not a school within a school. This isn't necessarily a bad thing, but it is not the original goal, which was to create a distinct learning environment such as those found in many highly successful charter or magnet schools.

There are exceptions to every rule, but the RPV theory seems to be an effective tool for analyzing educational innovations and making some predictions about their likelihood for success in a given learning organization. Without adequate resources, room to establish appropriate and new processes, and the ability to incubate the idea in a community that values it, such programs have a much lower chance of success. Get these three elements in place, though, and new ideas have a chance to succeed. While the RPV theory can't guarantee extraordinary outcomes, it at least allows the innovation fertile soil in which to grow.

Section II:
Knowing the Context and the People

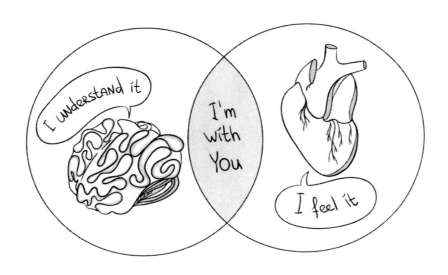

9

Why and How People Adopt Innovations

Often when we are thinking about what practices to promote and how to promote them, we fail to stop and recognize why people adopt new practices. With that in mind, I'd like to reflect on a number of tendencies that people have when it comes to the adoption of innovations in education. Recognizing that these are at play will give us a helpful perspective as we go about change management.

Head and Heart

As a rule, educators do not make decisions about how to teach, what teaching tools to use, or whether or not to adopt new methods and approaches because of some carefully reasoned or evidence-based strategy. While some educators might look to evidence-based research in their planning, other considerations such as instinct, folk knowledge, prior experience, attachment to certain traditions, and other similar factors often come into play as well.

Nonetheless, when a new idea or practice is proposed, some of these same people will challenge it and ask for evidence, research, and a well reasoned rationale. Even if you give them all of that, you might not accomplish what you hoped. Evidence, research, and reasoning are not the only influencers.

All of us have a unique mix of motives and rationales for how we teach and the tools we use. That is more often than not appropriate. Remembering that we all make choices with both our heads and our hearts can help us better understand others' reluctance to new ideas as well as their openness to new possibilities.

57

Art Versus Science

Is teaching an art or a science? The truth is, both spheres inform what teaching is and how it's done.

How do we determine if a teaching practice is scientifically sound? Even if we rigorously apply the scientific method to learning about an educational practice, we still leave room for discussion. A finding published in a scientific journal is not the end of the conversation about an idea, but only the beginning. Then begins the need for discourse, debate, and follow-up studies that eventually can amass into a body of helpful evidence that guides us toward a new best practice.

What about the art of teaching? Some argue that there is no absolute right or wrong when it comes to art, yet clearly there are standards for what constitutes good art and bad art. While people can disagree wildly about what they like and don't like in art, there are also largely accepted common understandings. For instance, most people can accurately judge that my attempt at ballet (since I have no formal training nor involvement beyond watching my daughter at ballet class on occasion) does not compare to a performance by Mikhail Baryshnikov.

Comparing one professional to another may be more nuanced and debatable. There is considerable room for debate, even among people who are in agreement about whether teaching is an art or a science. However, when educators or educational leaders spout opinions in this area before they have taken the time to learn the nuances and involve themselves in the broader discourse, they are somewhat akin to the person who flippantly dismisses online learning without doing the research or exploration that would earn a passing grade on a middle school research paper. In such situations, we must be firm and challenge ourselves to raise the bar on the expectations for what it means to be involved in the field of education.

Right and Wrong, or Benefits and Limitations?

Teachers have deep-seated beliefs and values that inform how they think and what they do in the classroom, making it easier for them to frame their positions on past, current, or emerging practices in moral or ethical terminology. Within these frameworks, one practice is right and the other is wrong; a certain technology is good while another is bad.

Generally, unless the discourse has to do with morals or ethics, it is more helpful to guide the conversation away from moral and ethical terminology and turn instead toward discussions about the benefits and limitations of a given practice or technology. What values does the practice or technology amplify or muffle? What benefits does it generate and what limitations or restrictions does it create? How are these answers similar or different in diverse contexts? Such questions will often highlight any number of important values and ethical considerations, but they also help us to venture into a much more nuanced and open conversation.

Nurture Openness to New Practices and Ideas

There is much that is malleable about us as humans, and much of my research and scholarship depends upon that premise. For example, I work from an assumption that people are able to become more curious and develop a greater love of learning, but I acknowledge, at the same time, that there are people who will not move in those directions.

Some people are, by nature, more curious than others, and the same is true about people's levels of openness to the new or the novel. When you are thinking about change management, it is important to remember this observation. You will never devise a perfect change management plan that produces total adoption at an even rate across all people, unless you are brilliant at stacking the deck through your hiring practices (which is a valid strategy in some cases).

Do People Use What They Like, or Do They Like What They Use?

Once people begin working through a new practice and there is broad adoption, they oftentimes come to prefer that which was adopted. Then, even if a more promising practice or technology comes along, people continue to prefer what they have already come to know. For some, that current practice took much work and emotional energy to adopt. They are finally comfortable with it and find it stressful to think of going through all that work again. Even the suggestion conjures anxiety. We are wise to keep this effort of change in mind. This doesn't mean we refrain from moving forward, but it might mean we guide people through the potential stress.

People Prefer the Familiar

The more original and creative your innovation, the more important it is to remember that people often prefer the familiar. In the research about the diffusion of innovation, this is a key consideration. It is one that will be helpful as you explore changes in your organization.

People tend to listen to and be more open with those with whom they feel similar, people with whom they can relate. If you come off as a rebel in the community, unless you have somehow earned an immense amount of trust from those in the community, people will be less likely to follow and consider your new ideas. I've learned this the hard way. I once had an early conversation with a colleague about my more radical views on education. It was so far from this person's own views and convictions that now, several years later, that person almost instantly assumes that any idea from me is radical, suspect, and best to leave unconsidered.

If you know you are perceived as a rebel, either find people who are "insiders" who will help with the innovation, or find ways to build rapport and become a more familiar and relatable figure. The same is true for the practice or innovation itself. If it is viewed as beyond the pale, people will have a more difficult time accepting it, at least in the beginning. Consider framing it in terms of how it is similar to what people already embrace or accept in some part of their life or work.

People Prefer What They Discovered

The more we can involve people in exploring the possibilities and selecting the direction, the easier it is to develop shared ownership. Consider how you can invite people behind the scenes, so that they can play a role in shaping the future. This approach can lead to a much faster adoption of a new practice as well as innovations that stick. If your organization is a startup, make sure you recruit and hire people who are on board with the key concepts of your innovation, people who have already discovered those concepts for themselves and are ready to join others who have come to the same conclusions and want to take action.

Consider how you can be really curious about people, about change management, and about the entire process. There are important sociological and psychological elements that affect the adoption of new practices and innovations. Ignore these nuances at your peril. Look, listen, learn, and use what you learn to build a community of trust and possibility.

10

Understanding Your Team's Proclivities for Educational Innovation

All of us have a wonderful blend of inherited traits that are constantly merging with those that grow out of life and experience. Using this fact as a starting point, I developed a framework for understanding human beings' different proclivities when it comes to educational change and innovation. Each person will approach innovation differently, so a varied approach that considers these differences increases our chances of success.

Different people tend to have different reactions to emerging models, approaches, and frameworks; some people are more prone to ask and value certain questions over others. For the purposes of this discussion, we can call those reactions and tendencies proclivities. As with many such frameworks, a person's reaction often arises from a blend of two or more of his or her proclivities, but one proclivity usually takes the lead while others play supporting roles.

Similarly, the context and nature of a community affects a person's proclivity for a particular context. A person might gravitate toward one proclivity in one part of his or her life but gravitate toward a different one in another group or community. Similarly, a person's proclivities change over time as their life experiences unfold. As we think about our own teams in learning organizations, consider how these proclivities are present and how recognizing them might allow us to manage change while valuing the unique contributions and perspectives of the different players on that team.

The Assumption Proclivity

Also known as the "first impression proclivity," the assumption proclivity is a tendency for a person to assume an understanding of the innovation, its benefits, and/or its drawbacks, and to make that assumption quickly. Sometimes this tendency is based on that person's having extensive experience in a related area, as often such experience will allow one to make a quick and correct judgment about the innovation or change.

In the world of online learning, I see the assumption proclivity quite often. Generally, it comes from people who have quick opinions about the educational value of online learning in general. It also comes from people who have training and experience with one approach to online learning and come to believe in that approach and certain practices related to that approach as nonnegotiable best practices, labeling approaches and practices outside of that realm of experience as wrong or uninformed. On the other hand, the assumption proclivity can also just as easily lead a person to assume that a given innovation is excellent and to be certain that innovation is the way to go. Such thinking often comes from a mindset that "new is better."

As with all proclivities, there are benefits and limitations to this one. The downside of the assumption proclivity is demonstrated when people are overbearing or unwilling to bracket their first reaction long enough to develop a deeper and more substantive understanding of the innovation. The benefit of having a person with an assumption proclivity is that these people can help spark a lively and even powerful conversation, especially if there are enough people engaged in the conversation who have other proclivities and that there is enough trust within the group.

The Skeptical Proclivity

The person with the skeptical proclivity (also referred to as the Thomas proclivity) treats educational innovations and changes as guilty until proven innocent. This proclivity sometimes comes from having lived through countless educational fads and perceiving them as largely ineffective or even damaging. In other instances, it comes from a desire for positive evidence to support any change or innovation. While these people sometimes come off as negative, they can be valuable in helping to refine an idea and to genuinely evaluate its worth.

The Wait-and-See Proclivity

Distinct from the skeptical proclivity, the wait-and-see proclivity is a tendency for a person to sit back and watch when a new innovation is introduced. This person does not appear to make a judgment either in favor of or in opposition to an innovation, but at the same time, neither does the person show a desire to scrutinize it, leaving such examination for others. If the innovation takes root and gains momentum, this person is likely to follow suit and will make the best of it, but he or she will not be an early adopter (as described in Everett Rogers' work on the *Diffusion of Innovation*). On the other hand, they won't be laggards. Instead, depending upon the circumstance, they tend to join in with the early or late adopters.

The Analytical Proclivity

The analytical proclivity is also distinct from the skeptical proclivity, although people with this proclivity can often be mistaken as skeptical. This proclivity is the tendency to dissect the change or innovation, wanting to explore it from different angles and move forward or resist it with a clear and deep understanding of its benefits and limitations. Sometimes the person with the analytical proclivity sounds negative because she or he is willing to genuinely look at and entertain strong criticisms. However, this person analyzes a new idea with the intention of understanding it rather than destroying it. In postmodern terminology, these are not deconstructionists in the sense that they want to tear the idea apart and leave it laying on the ground. They want to tear it apart and then put it back together, sometimes making wonderfully helpful enhancements along the way, enhancements that can mitigate some of the limitations of the change or innovation.

The Possibility Proclivity

The person with the possibility proclivity has similarities both to those with the assumption proclivity (in the positive sense) and those with the analytical proclivity. The person with the possibility proclivity analyzes the change or innovation quickly by jumping to its benefits and possibilities. "What are the possibilities that would emerge with this change or innovation?" they ask. Essentially these people are analytical and focus almost exclusively on an innovation's benefits. Sometimes these people appear to have a belief that innovations are inevitable and that it is important to figure out how to make the best of them, use them for the greatest benefit, or amplify a given value. For people with the possibility proclivity, engaging with an innovation is an exercise in imagination and creativity.

The Doomsday Proclivity

The doomsday proclivity is the flip side of the possibility proclivity. People with the doomsday proclivity tend to imagine the worst-case scenarios. However, given encouragement from a trusting community, these team members can be encouraged to bolster their proclivity to imagine the worst with a strong secondary proclivity to consider positive possibilities as well as negative ones. While the doomsday proclivity may sound like an unpleasant perspective, people with this proclivity often have passionate concerns and can help to elevate the group's understanding of genuine risks that should be managed as part of a given change or innovation. Ignore their concerns and they may leave or become silent or outspoken resisters.

The Big Picture Proclivity

The big picture proclivity is the tendency to put a given change or innovation into perspective by thinking about larger overall organizational or community goals and needs. It is a mindset that may accept a less-than-perfect innovation because the person sees that innovation as moving the organization or community in the right direction. Likely, they anticipate being able to adjust or redirect at a later time as needed.

The Moral Good Proclivity

People with the moral good proclivity tend to view changes and innovations as either good or bad. While these people may have tendencies that overlap the other proclivities, they have strong moral and ethical sensibilities, and they seek to evaluate a given change quickly by a set of moral beliefs or convictions. People with other proclivities advocate a moral code as well, but people with the moral good proclivity have a tendency to make a moral judgment the first of their evaluations. These people try to decide, first of all, if this is the right thing to do and if it helps to support a core set of values and convictions. I often see this proclivity in an educator who has a clear and personally compelling personal mission that drives his or her actions and decisions as an educator. That mission might be a core value like the belief that everyone has a right to a good education, the value of human agency, and the value of developing deep and positive relationships with each learner, or a belief in the importance of treating each student as precious and full of potential.

The What-Does-This-Mean-For-Me Proclivity

As you can guess from the name, the what-does-this-mean-for-me proclivity is a tendency to evaluate innovations and changes based on how they will harm or benefit the person. A person with this proclivity will evaluate an innovation first on whether it means more or less work for him or her, requires changing ingrained habits or relearning a great deal, or if it will affect the person's other life commitments. While this proclivity may seem selfish to some, it can also be seen as simply counting the cost. People in education, like those in any field, need to have boundaries, and this proclivity is the tendency to assess changes based upon whether the person is willing or able to invest in a given change or innovation.

Note that people with this proclivity are not necessarily asking, "What is in it for me?" although they could be. Instead, these people are trying to figure out what an innovation means for them. These people may decide that it means a great deal of work and change, but it is worth it nonetheless. They may decide the opposite as well. The point here is that these people are first driven to figure out the personal effect of a given change.

Note that I do not describe any of these proclivities as wrong or inappropriate. In fact, in most contexts I tend to see it as helpful to have people with a wide range of proclivities. Such diversity, when experienced in the context of a trusting community, makes for wonderfully rich and valuable discussions. Of course, given their differences, people are seeking answers to different questions. As much as a leader or change agent might want to get everyone focused upon asking and answering the same set of questions, because people have these different proclivities, such a unified focus seldom occurs. Delineating these proclivities in this way can give us a glimpse into what could be happening in the minds of the different people in the group. Understanding, recognizing, and respecting the value of the different questions that come with each proclivity allow us to manage change in a way that honors and benefits from the unique blend of genes and experiences within the team.

11

Helping the Reluctant to Learn from Educational Extremes

Most people who choose to become educators don't do so because they love change, innovation, and entrepreneurial efforts. Instead, most educators choose to go into education because they love the content or discipline they teach; they love teaching students and having a positive effect on students' lives; they love schooling as they know or knew it; they want to make a positive contribution to society; or they adhere to some combination of these reasons.

Most educators who work in K-12 schools or institutions of higher education are working in a largely traditional context, one that dabbles with trends and innovations but which remains largely consistent from year to year, decade to decade, even century to century. On the other hand, many educators recognize that we are in a time of unprecedented educational change and innovation. That notion can be uncomfortable, and educators often struggle with how to respond to these changes.

This struggle can be heightened when educators are introduced to changes they perceive as radical. Innovations such as Massive Open Online Courses (MOOCs), online learning, digital badges for learning, self-directed learning, project-based learning, and competency-based education can seem so extreme to people who value traditional ways of doing things that they dismiss those innovations without examination. However, given time to explore, dabble, experiment, candidly discuss and critique, and have some final say on the extent to which they embrace certain changes, most educators are open to incremental change. Nonetheless, barriers remain, and here is a list of some of them.

A Heightened Sense of Fear and Uncertainty

Change provokes fear for many, and in time of fear, people are less open to considering new things. When we are fearful, we tend to see things in terms of black and white or right and wrong, and our responses can become a quick yes or no, with no consideration of the nuances or the gray versions of the idea. For instance, when educators first learned about MOOCs from the media, early responses were that they might replace higher education institutions, that they could jeopardize their jobs, and that they had an immense dropout rate. Such complaints are enough to scare many people who work in education.

Those of us who truly study MOOCs, however, know that these are black-and-white claims and that the power and possibility of MOOCs lies in the grays. While a sense of urgency can be a powerful lever for prompting change in organizations, including schools, there is no need for a sense of fearful urgency with regard to MOOCs. Such fear tactics merely serve to crush creativity and disable flexibility.

The Other

Ample research shows that people are less likely to adopt innovations or changes when those changes are championed by someone considered to be outside their peer group. If we notice that educators and other education stakeholders label proponents of a given innovation as "the other," then we have our work cut out for us. Then comes the work of helping those educators to find common ground with the innovators, experiencing them as real people and not straw men or caricatures, and discovering people with whom they can relate. Until that work has been accomplished, little else will move forward.

The Same Old Same Old

Those who have been working in education for any longer than a decade have been bombarded with numerous educational trends and innovations during that time. Add a new one and they will be tempted to dismiss it quickly as just one more attempt at improving education, and just as likely to fail as all the others they have seen. What is really required is a fair assessment of the new innovations. What is old? What is new?

The Hard Sell

Advocates of a new idea can come off as blind to any flaws in a new idea. They talk about it as if it were their newborn infant, beautiful beyond imagination. This attitude can trigger suspicion from others, sometimes causing them to be unwilling even to consider the idea. A more balanced approach recognizes that all educational innovations and practices, both the old and the new, have benefits and drawbacks, affordances and limitations. A sense of balance on the part of the advocates offers a chance for candid conversations about what is best for the learning organization and its students.

One-Sided Versions

Mainstream news sources and even the more grassroots blogs are filled with misrepresentations of emerging trends and innovations in education. If you follow my blog (www.etale.org), then you've read my responses to such misrepresentations about everything from MOOCs to the Common Core State Standards Initiative. I am deeply concerned that a steady diet of these media misrepresentations will inhibit honest exploration and experimentation with new ideas, and I am all the more concerned because exploration and experimentation are vital for helping schools and learning organizations improve.

We must develop a critical eye, take the time to review things from multiple perspectives, and recognize that some people who write about educational innovations on the Internet, especially on the news sites, are often writing without a strong insider's perspective or from a single insider's perspective. While this is not always the case, very often it is.

Take MOOCs as an example. How many writers post articles about MOOCs as if Coursera and EdX were the only two providers out there? This movement in open learning is much more diverse than such flawed articles would suggest. To help people become comfortable with exploring new ideas, we have to find ways to offer more multi-faceted perspectives on the issues, not one-sided views. In addition, we need people who are willing to critique as well as promote the innovations.

Time and Interest

Educators are busy people with priorities in work and life. Not all—not even most—of them get energized by spending hours analyzing every new idea, especially when there are an overwhelming number of new ideas. Innovation fatigue is real, even for those who are trying to be open to the trends and possibilities.

This predicament calls for a reasonable and understanding response. First, do we want every educator to become a trend chaser and innovation analyst? Or are we better off empowering each educator to major in his or her strengths and passions for the sake of education? While it is reasonable to expect educators to stay current in their field, moderation can be a powerful tool for helping educators and others to make progress toward analyzing and integrating worthwhile innovations. It is good to have a small core group that loves to scout for useful innovations. This team can share ideas with the rest of the staff for consideration, but don't expect everyone to become a scout.

12

Educational Innovation that Moves Mountains

Ben Franklin wrote, "All mankind is divided into three classes: those that are immovable, those that are movable, and those that move."

I read Ben Franklin's autobiography almost every year, so when I ran across this Franklin quote in the last chapter of *Creative Schools: The Grassroots Revolution That's Transforming Education*, by Ken Robinson and Lou Aronica, I took notice. The authors applied this quote to education, providing important insights about educational innovation, change management, and education reform. Here I build on these ideas, putting an autobiographical spin on them.

"The Immovable"

Immovable people are largely set in their ways. They ignore, don't see, or resist the need for change. The authors refer to them as boulders in a stream that the water rushes around, and they suggest that we not invest our time in trying to move them. Change is constant and they will, unfortunately, be left behind.

I consult with organizations that are grappling with change, and in that role I consider this sage advice, but sometimes the reality is more complex than the book's simple metaphor would suggest. What if the boulder is the person in charge or the one who controls the purse strings? What if the boulders are parents who resist or deny the need for change because the change in question is not similar to something they have experienced? What if there are wonderfully gifted and effective boulders? What if the boulders are policymakers and regulators? What if there is a seemingly impenetrable row of boulders in your way? To complicate matters even further, I've noticed that sometimes people can be only part boulder, open to and embracing of change in some areas but entrenched in others.

It is not always apparent which people are the boulders. I've seen wonderfully gifted people be labeled as boulders by one group seeking change in a certain direction, and then embraced as a true mover and change agent when they are working with a different group, which is seeking to bring about a very different change. Even in my own large and wonderfully complex organization, it is not uncommon to have two groups, each of which embraces a bold and noble vision, clashes with one another, and labels the other as less noble or even immovable. We must recognize that there are wildly different personalities in the world, and some will clash and conflict, even though each can make a remarkable contribution to a noble mission.

"The Movable"

Movable people are those who see that change is coming. They might even recognize the need to do things differently, but they are not likely the ones to lead the way. As Michael Crow once stated about universities that are stuck in the industrial age, movable people are desperately in need of exemplars, people who, with help and support, can participate in bringing about the necessary changes. I have a persistent hope that people are movable, that they are willing to be reasonable, even supportive, given the right conditions. Fear, love, uncertainty, lack of confidence or myriad thoughts and emotions make it difficult for them to take effective action for change.

I gained compassion for movable people when I experienced a panic attack in my late thirties. I had no idea what was happening at the time, and it was astonishing to me how the attack's associated fear limited my ability to think creatively, imagine possibilities, and embrace change. For a short time I despaired. What do you do with a man who has lived and breathed educational innovation for years but suddenly experiences fear at the slightest change? It took months to work through that fear, but I now consider it an extraordinary gift. That experience provided me with a level of empathy that I could have never imagined. It also gave me a wondrous hope for even the most seemingly immovable people. As a teacher reminded me more than 25 years ago when I was going through a difficult time early in life, "This, too, will pass."

People can change, and sometimes it is possible to have the honor of helping them embrace an important educational reform. At the same time, there are limits. Ultimately, education is about the learning and the learners, and someone who persistently resists required change can't be prioritized above these other two. I don't want to go to a hospital that tolerates doctors who resist current and research-based practices in lieu of preferences and an insistence on using flawed and outdated practices. The same is true in education, even though what is best practice in education can sometimes be more debatable than best practice in medicine.

At some point, we need to leave the dock in pursuit of the vision, bringing along those who are willing to join us. This means leaving others behind and recognizing that still others will opt to take their own ship on a different journey. As Thomas Edison is credited with saying, "Vision without execution is hallucination." There comes a time to act, and time will not stand still or wait for anyone.

"Those who Move"

Those who move are the leaders, innovators, and change agents, people who have a vision for a better future and act to make their vision a reality. As Robinson and Aronica wrote, these people "know that they don't always need permission."

He explained that these are the people who, collectively, are capable of bringing about a much-needed educational revolution.

Not everyone is going to be a mover. In fact, I tend to think that most organizations and communities can benefit by having a variety of people on this spectrum. At the same time, if you have ever had the privilege of witnessing or participating in a group or community of movers fixated on the same vision who have the resources they need, and who are hard at work, then you have experienced a truly powerful force, one that is strong enough to move a mountain of boulders.

13

Building a Plane in the Air

Is making educational change like building an airplane in the air?

I once had the privilege of assisting with a boot camp for a select group of schools that had been chosen to get help with working toward a school-wide make-over. The boot camp focused on moving the schools toward a blended learning model that amplified their core values. The goal was to help these schools be successful with this innovation while also developing promising practices that could be shared and replicated elsewhere.

We started the first day with a critical conversation about the compelling reason behind each of the schools' philosophies, continuing the conversation with a discussion about having nonnegotiable school-shaping concepts through which they could sift new programs, projects, ideas, policies, and practices. Without such groundwork, it is far too easy for blended learning to become a case of chasing the next shiny thing. As I explained in the chapters on mission-driven innovation and traits of innovative schools, coming up with your organization's school-shaping concepts and making them truly nonnegotiable are key steps to creating a mission-minded educational innovation that pops, one that has a distinct and compelling identity and that results in a highly effective learning organization.

At the end of that first day when we debriefed, I was struck and excited by a question from one of the participants: "I see how you can do this if you are starting a new school or doing a restart, but some of us are not in a position to do that. How do we make changes now, while we are still teaching students and working through many of the identity questions?"

The question points to an important truth. School-wide educational innovations in existing organizations require rigorous change management and a fine sense of timing. Leaders need to know when, what, how, and how much to adjust at any given time. Making sweeping changes to an existing school is the equivalent of building (or at least updating) an airplane in the air.

Some guiding principles can help to highlight the risks associated with such efforts and guide change agents toward success:

Changing Course

Usually, you are not building or rebuilding the concept of "school." You are just adjusting or changing course. Course corrections are not uncommon for airplanes in the air; pilots do so routinely. We often need to adapt to changing circumstances, and that is why such things as curricula require continual review and adjustment. When we make course corrections, we're not so much building a new plane as making necessary adjustments, as a good airplane pilot would do when flying a plane.

Major Changes Are Made on the Ground, When People Are Not Present

When an airplane needs major maintenance, it's done on the ground, and so it is with schools too. Major changes typically happen between school years, often with the planning for the change taking place during one school year, but launching during the next. There are exceptions, of course, but not even the best mechanic would attempt to build an airplane engine while the plane was in the air. Some things can be worked on as you go, but it just isn't possible or advisable to make core changes while your plane or your school is in the air.

Building and Rebuilding Require Care and Skill

Whether on the ground or in the air, it takes time, skill, and special attention to build and rebuild, and to do so in a way that does no harm. Success in building and rebuilding will require knowing the difference between a major change and a minor adjustment. It also requires having the wisdom to choose the best strategy to make the changes and achieve the goals.

Education Innovation Is Not a One-Person Task

If you have a small and simple enough team or organization, some changes can be led and managed by a single person, but most learning organizations don't work that way. There are many aspects to leading a successful educational innovation, and a committed, cooperative, core team is going to be necessary.

While these suggestions may seem simple, I've seen plenty of instances where innovations or attempted changes failed because lessons like these were ignored. Lone ranger efforts rarely work in complex learning organizations. Changes without a clear goal and a compelling reason behind them often don't have what it takes to persist or last. Before the intended innovation can be accomplished, a learning curve is usually required, along with the need to develop or tap special expertise.

Building in the air is sometimes doable and advisable. Other times we are wise to wait until we land to work on the next big innovation. It is important to assess what we can do "in the air" and what needs to wait until we are back on the ground. Pay attention to the suggestions here and you will greatly increase your chances for a successful rebuild.

14

"I Already Tried That"

Whatever field you're in, whether education or any other, you have no doubt experienced something like the following. An administrator or professional development facilitator encourages, or maybe even requires, a teacher to implement a new practice or strategy. The teacher tries it and runs into problems, so he or she returns to previous practice. When asked about the new practice or strategy, the person explains that he or she tried it and it didn't work. "I already tried that," the teacher says.

While it might make sense to some that the teacher was making a logical choice by returning to old ways of doing things, I'm not so sure such a strategy makes sense for the long term. Consider the following four scenarios:

Physical Therapy Treatment

A person is recovering from an injury and the doctor encourages the person to work with a physical therapist. The person goes the first time, and the physical therapist takes him or her through a series of stretches and strengthening exercises. The therapy session is painful, but the person gets through it. However, the patient goes home and never returns. When asked why he or she didn't return, the person explains that it was painful, and the therapy didn't do anything to improve the condition.

Piano Lessons

A person decides to learn to play the piano. The person finds a teacher, goes to a first lesson, becomes embarrassed because of how little he knows, and then quits. When asked why, the person explains that the lessons were not working. "I tried to play the piano, but it didn't work." Would we have a single concert pianist in the world if this were the common attitude?

Reading a Classic

You are in a literature class that is reading T.S. Eliot's *The Waste Land*. You read it through once, become completely confused and then give up, explaining that this poem doesn't make any sense. Plenty of people of people do this, but they miss out on the joy of discovering rich meaning and nuance.

Learning to Drive a Car

You start driver's education and have your first lesson driving a car. As you start to pull out of the parking lot, the engine makes strange noises and shuts down. You try to restart it but have no luck. You and the teacher check under the hood, but there is no obvious solution. So you quit driver's education, explaining to everyone that driving is not good because the technology isn't reliable.

We read these examples and easily see the errors in thinking. Of course you are not usually going to get better after a single physical therapy treatment. Of course you are unable to play the piano well after a single lesson. Of course it will take multiple readings and some research to understand a poem like *The Waste Land*. Of course driving works, but this person just had a bad experience. Yet, when it comes to educational innovation, exploring new practices and methods, I've observed a similar line of thinking countless times.

The person taking or teaching a blended or online course for the first time has a bad experience and uses that as evidence that all blended and online learning is bad or ineffective or that the technology is unreliable. Or a teacher tries teaching a certain type of blended learning class, doesn't enjoy it and quits, similar to the person who doesn't enjoy practicing playing the piano before he or she can play a song. Nonetheless, that teacher will explain to anyone who cares to listen that the teaching method in question is a bad one.

A person tries to design and teach her first project-based learning lesson and it bombs. She concludes that project-based learning doesn't work with her students or maybe not at all. Someone invites a teacher to replace a lecture-dominant approach to teaching with a Socratic method. The questions are not well crafted as the teacher has not yet developed skills with Socratic teaching, and the class doesn't perform as well on the first exam. The teacher concludes that lecture is clearly a superior teaching method to Socratic teaching.

Implementing something new often takes study, practice, time, multiple attempts, reflection, revision, and ongoing adjustments. Of all people, shouldn't educators be the first to understand this process? A teaching method is not like a pill you take that instantly makes you feel better. It almost always needs to be combined with the development of new knowledge and skills. Even then, it is accompanied by ongoing reflective practice to refine the craft. Such an understanding is really a foundational element of being an effective learner.

Notice what happens when people approach new strategies, methods, and models with an ongoing commitment to working hard at it, bringing curiosity, reflective practice, and an understanding that, for instance, you don't make a great surgeon by giving a doctor a great method. Only the development of accompanying skills can allow for a great method to give great results. The same is true in teaching and learning. We need educators—and learners—who embrace such a mindset.

15

Understanding the Adopters of Educational Innovation

How do you promote the adoption of an innovation in your learning organization?

If you've seen the term "early adopter," then you have at least a passing acquaintance with the work of Everett Rogers, author of a 1962 text, *The Diffusion of Innovation*, that helped to explain how innovation gets adopted in various communities or cultures. Even though newer models and theories abound, Rogers' work remains a classic that continues to shape the way we think and talk about technology and the adoption of innovation. His framework remains a useful resource for anyone who is thinking about managing change and promoting a promising innovation in any organization, including a learning organization.

Rogers divided adopters into six categories based on the timing of their adoption, their role in a broader adoption, and the extent to which they ever adopt. There are the innovators, early adopters, early majority, late majority, laggards, and the leapfroggers. The following is a short explanation of these six categories.

Innovators

Innovators are people who have the resources and risk tolerance necessary for creating innovations, including those that eventually gain wider adoption. Failure is common and an understood part of their work. Innovators are people who have access not only to what is necessary for bringing a particular new idea into physical reality but also know how to go about creating that innovation, often tapping into the best and most current research.

Early Adopters

Early adopters are thought leaders and others who have a high level of respect from many others. They don't take as many risks as the innovators and are judicious in what they adopt, but their influential role should not be overlooked.

Early Majority

Individuals in the early majority are often connected to the early adopters, but they do not hold positions of thought leadership.

Late Majority

The late majority typically has no connection with either innovators or early adopters. These people approach innovations with a measure of skepticism and adopt innovations a little later than the average person does. They also have limited access to any thought leadership around the innovation.

Laggards

As the name would suggest, laggards are the last people to adopt an innovation. They are not well connected to people in the other groups, are champions for tradition and the status quo, and usually have little to no influence on others when it comes to adoption.

Leapfroggers

Leapfroggers hold out on a given innovation, often through several iterations, but eventually do adopt it.

About the Six Categories

Notice the relationships among the different adopting groups. For instance, innovators do not directly influence laggards, because laggards tend to interact only with other laggards and people in the late majority. The way to influence laggards is through people in the late majority; even the most compelling case from an innovator will probably not embolden laggards to consider something new.

Innovators influence other innovators and early adopters. Early adopters influence other early adopters and the early majority. You get the idea. This approach is not a perfect science and there are many exceptions, but the general concept is important for anyone wishing to effect change: People tend to be influenced more by those with whom they can relate and with whom they share much in common. This is an important foundation upon which to think about how we promote the adoption of new ideas. Once we have these ideas in mind, we can be far more systematic and effective in our strategies to promote the adoption of an innovation.

16

Embrace Wonderfully Lopsided People

Embrace those people I like to think of as "wonderfully lopsided," giving them freedom to develop their strengths while helping them to minimize or manage their limitations.

Some educational organizations appear to idolize the well-rounded person, the employee equivalent of the student who gets straight As in all subjects, plays multiple sports, and is loved by everyone. If you only look for those people, you are going to miss out on some world-class talent. There is a reason why many great leaders and innovators throughout history were not those straight A students.

Some of the best people in the world are wonderfully lopsided. They have one or a few huge strengths, and they build on those strengths and use them to do extraordinary things. They also have gaps and limitations. You can either focus on those limitations or you can embrace the whole person and help them to manage their limitations while letting them do amazing things in the organization with their strengths. But if you push them only to work on their weaknesses you risk preventing them from creating their next masterpiece.

Create Spaces for Freedom, Experimentation, and Exploration

Organizations often have accepted, even "acceptable," ways of doing things, standard practices and policies that can squelch innovation. Innovators and entrepreneurs need freedom to breathe, to move, and to experiment, but many learning organizations have fixed mindsets and well established cultures that target earnings alone. Experimentation, by its very nature, has uncertain results, and is therefore discouraged in these organizations.

If you want to encourage innovation in your organization, then you'll need to develop a tolerance for uncertainty and learn to celebrate experimentation, because without experimentation and its inherent uncertainty you will probably not get much world-class innovation. It can take months or years for some innovative experiments to yield benefits, but if you have the resources and patience to wait for the results, your organization could reap huge dividends. While you don't need to allow lavish spending on risky ventures that might spell doom for your organization, you can learn to manage risks that you deem reasonable and tolerable for your organization's culture.

Don't Change the Rules in the Middle of the Game

Top-down power moves, such as changing the rules in the middle of the game, instill fear throughout an organization.

Fear can be a motivator, but it also kills motivation and saps energy from most innovators and entrepreneurs. Threats, top-down power plays, and autocratic changes behind closed doors will send your top talent running. While you'll keep the rule followers and those people who are satisfied to follow directives from above, you'll lose your innovators and entrepreneurs almost every time.

Imagine someone interrupting a game of chess you're playing by jumping in and pulling some of your pieces off the board, forcing you to play without those pieces. Then imagine that person changes the rules of the game, right then and there. You'd probably stand up and walk away. In the same way, that unpredictability will squash the spirits of innovative people and teams in your organization.

"Equal Treatment" Is a Myth

You might believe that you're treating all people and all units in your organization equally, but they don't all need the same things at the same time. Instead, look for ways to invest in promising ideas and people who are working on the next innovation. Find ways to fund, support, and empower those people while helping the rest of the organization to see the wisdom and importance of supporting such strategies.

Quite often you'll find that you will need to give your idea people and innovators freedom and flexibility to operate outside the boundaries, allowing them the option of doing things that might not usually be done. They might be things that do not fit with standard policies and practices. There is a careful line to draw here. Some things are nonnegotiable, but learn to be flexible when you can.

Don't Expect Innovators and Entrepreneurs to Color Within the Lines

This tip is similar to the previous one. If you want to embrace a culture of innovation and entrepreneurship, then you'll need to realize that innovative people often don't color within the lines. Accepting their proclivities in this regard can be a challenge, because coloring between the lines was pretty much invented in schools. If you want to pursue true educational innovation, it is time to let go of this school rule.

Be Open to Change While Remaining True to Your Mission

Sift new ideas through the filter of your mission and vision, but be open to interesting twists and improvisations, even around the mission and vision.

The mission, vision, values, and goals that are central to the organization need to be standard for all people, even the innovators, and the lines around them should be nonnegotiable. All the same, while the innovators in particular need to respect, embrace, and innovate around the mission and vision, if those people are given freedom from some of the traditional trappings, they could delight you with surprising variations on how that vision appears to them. Too often we confuse the "how" of what we do with "why" we do it. Give freedom to innovate around the "how" and watch the mission get amplified by your educational innovators.

Network Carefully

Partner, network, connect, beg, borrow, and steal (in the flattering, not the illegal sense), but beware of disengaged outsourcing.

Outsourcing part of your operation can be an effective strategy at times, but stay deeply engaged while you do so. Remain cautious, but be cognizant that some of the best people in the world are not a part of your organization. Partner, connect, and network with those people. At a minimum, try to learn from the best people, organizations, and innovations in the world. Learn as much as you can from them, and try to build on your own intellectual capital in the process.

Section III:
Knowing the Tips and Tricks

17

Infuse Your Learning Organization with a Spirit of Innovation and Entrepreneurship

In *Bold: How to Go Big, Create Wealth, and Impact the World*, Peter H. Diamandis and Steven Kotler wrote, "If you don't disrupt yourself someone else will." While this statement is not an absolute, it is certainly a proverbial truth. It is applicable to innovation in education as well as to any other entrepreneurial endeavor.

Today's education space is one of tremendous innovation and entrepreneurship. This doesn't mean we should abandon every practice or tradition, and given that education is a collective social good, it doesn't even mean that every learning organization needs to be deeply innovative and entrepreneurial. There is plenty of room for different types of learning organizations from kindergarten through higher education, and also in the massive education space that lies beyond these formal organizations.

However, if you aspire to lead an innovative and entrepreneurial organization, you will probably need to make a few changes, both in yourself and in your organization. There are plenty of ways to nurture a culture of innovation, and the tips that follow are only a few of them. Think of these tips as a way to get yourself started, not a recipe that you will follow to the letter. Not a single one of them is something you can do and check off as if you were completing a to-do list. Each one takes time, organizational and individual soul-searching, persistence, a thick skin, and a fervent commitment to the task.

Celebrate Innovation and Entrepreneurship

Don't just talk about innovation and entrepreneurship. Celebrate missional innovations. Lift them up. Encourage the qualities of the entrepreneur and innovator among people in your organization. Back up your encouragement with the necessary resources so that people feel confident about engaging in innovative and entrepreneurial activities.

Ensure that support for innovation comes from the very top. While the highest-ranking people in your organization don't need to lead the way, they do need to be seen to be as endorsing innovative efforts, and they need to celebrate entrepreneurial people and projects. One of the things this means for those in authority is that they need to give people space to be innovative. Entrepreneurs and innovators wither with micromanagement. Instead, they need support, accountability, encouragement, celebration, and empowerment.

Find People Who Are Passionate About Possibility

Hire or raise up people who are passionate about being deeply informed about the possibilities. C. E. M. Joad wrote, "The height of originality is skill in concealing origins." Great innovators do not just benchmark from and imitate similar organizations. That is often a trait of the uncertain and insecure. However, great innovators and entrepreneurs do study and learn from varied sources, even ones overlooked by most others working in a given field.

Ideation and innovation are both fueled by a deep and broad sense of the possibilities. There is a certain breed of person who craves exploring and discovering possibilities. Sometimes such people appear to be obsessed with discovering diverse sources, models, examples, and frameworks. They read and observe; they connect. They seem to know that they are building a deep well of insights from which they can draw when they begin to innovate.

These people are valuable to have around if you want a culture of innovation. Find people who are interested in more than merely replicating and imitating what other organizations do, or as Joad says, "concealing origins." Look for people who can keep the mission of your organization in focus while still exploring, in the most interdisciplinary or multidisciplinary way, the world for ideas, some of which could have an interesting application in your organization.

Match Entrepreneurs with People Who Get Things Done

Match entrepreneurs, innovators, and educational entrepreneurs with people who love being part of innovation and who are great at making things happen and attending to the details. (Read more about that eccentric breed of educator, the edupreneur, in a later chapter.) Don't make the mistake of adding detail people who are intimidated, overwhelmed, or even defensive about innovation, as that simply will not work out. Sometimes a person with an entrepreneurial bent is also someone with an eye for detail and a drive for impeccable completion, but this is not always the case. However, if you can match your innovators with people who have an eye for detail along with a taste for innovation and the drive to get things done and do them well, watch out! This can be a powerful combination.

Include Systems Thinkers

When you start to innovate, all sorts of things can be affected. Therefore it is extremely valuable to have people who understand all parts of the operation. These are people who sometimes live between the gaps of various offices and departments in an organization. At minimum, they think about how these groups interact, clash, connect, and impact one another.

Systems thinkers think about more than how one thing affects another within the organization. These people get under the hood. They want to know all aspects of the operation, and they don't just play or dabble. They dig deep, but they don't mistake their digging for full-scale expertise. They are vitally important resources, because they provide an understanding of what will work and what will not, or they lead the way toward conditions in which something new can work.

Oftentimes, the organization obsessed with specialists and tidy divisions of labor overlooks the wisdom of systems thinkers, with disastrous results. Systems thinkers see things that others just don't see. If a systems thinker has a track record of using his or her capacity for systems thinking to get things done well, trust the person with it.

And if you find an innovator who is also a systems thinker, grab that person and empower him or her. Many leaders who try to reorganize systems in an organization often do so with a narrow understanding of the implications. Yet, if you pair that leader with an entrepreneurial systems thinker, and that leader has the openness and humility to listen and learn from such a thinker, it can empower that leader to reshape the organization or aspects of the organization in incredibly positive ways.

18

Where and How to Start with Educational Innovation

Are you intrigued by the idea of working as an educational innovator or entrepreneur, but you're wondering how to get started? The following ideas are intended to give you a boost.

Start with Why

In a talk at the 2014 *ASU GSV Education Innovation Summit*, Steve Case said, "You really need to believe that you are onto something important."

Educational innovation has to be about more than money, the joy of scaling something, or simply increasing the number of students, products, or clients your innovation draws in. If you want to innovate with soul, then that means starting with a deep and compelling reason, as I've mentioned in previous chapters. This is such a central concept that I'm compelled to repeat it a few times in the book. Why do you want to innovate in a particular area? Don't skip over or cut corners on this piece of your work, as it is foundational. Your answers to this question will make a big difference for your health and well-being, the people around you, and the people who will hopefully benefit from your innovation.

Get Informed About the Possibilities and Innovate from Depth

I see many learning organizations stifled by the simple fact that they are unaware of wonderfully promising possibilities that can help them with their mission. Take the time to explore and learn about these possibilities. You don't have to like, embrace, or use everything you learn. Just get informed. Without this important element, one that I'm also planning to repeat often in this book, you will continually revert to past practices or a narrow set of options.

Build Your Personal Learning Network

If you want to explore innovation in a particular idea, add 10 to 20 people, communities, and resources to your personal learning network that will feed and inspire your work in this area. Who are the best and brightest in the world in this area? How can you learn from them and connect with them? Of course, be a good digital citizen and be more than a taker. Give, share, and assist those in your new network as well.

Challenge the Can't

Remember that common example of the elephant with a chain around his foot? After an elephant comes to believe that the chain is tied to a stake, he stops trying to fight it. Eventually, he will remain in a set area if someone simply puts a chain around his foot, even when the chain is not tied to a stake.

I know nothing about elephants, and I don't know if this technique actually works, but I see its equivalent in learning organizations all the time. We are restrained by what we think is not possible. Challenge that thinking. Be courageous enough to engage in some thought experiments, at least, and question whether certain assumed "essentials" are really valuable and if they support your mission.

Once I provided group consulting for a dozen school administrators. They wanted me to simply be available for a time of questions and answers. As we started, I asked them an important question. What are your non-negotiables? If I was going to spend a couple hours with them, I didn't want to waste their time by suggesting ideas that they were unwilling to consider. At first, they did not say much. A couple of people even shared that they are open to most anything. I tested that with a few questions. What about getting rid of letter grades in your school? What about changing the class schedules? What about adjusting your funding model? After six or seven such questions it became apparent that they were not willing to reconsider any of these areas. "We can't possibly change that," people stated. If we want to pursue missional innovation, we must challenge the can't.

Put Current Practices and Traditions into Perspective With Historical Inquiry

A study of history often reveals that traditions we think of as central in our educational institutions have far less historical basis than we thought. Letter grades, core curricula, school schedules, and other requirements that are often seen as fundamental all fall into this category. Dive into the history a bit. It will give you a longer view of things and help you to realize that even our most historic institutions have experienced significant changes over time.

Understand the Load-Bearing Walls

Remove a load-bearing wall in a house without reinforcing it first, and the house could fall on top of you. The same is true about changes in our institutions. This is a lesson I learned from Charles Schwahn and Beatrice McGarvey in their book, *Inevitable: Mass Customized Learning: Learning in an Age of Empowerment* . Find out what policies and practices are holding up the roof of the organization, and be sure to take precautions if your innovation will challenge one of those areas. Some innovations require removing or adjusting load-bearing walls. You can do it, but it takes great time and care. It is not an innovation that you can do overnight without massive implications, even some that impact your own career or tenure at the organization. In other instances, you will find that you can pursue an innovation while leaving a load-bearing wall intact. That will allow you to move much more quickly.

Look for Problems in the World

Get inspired by one of the world's problems, and innovate to help. This tip gives you your "why."

Great innovations address important problems. Keep this in mind as you consider educational innovations. As Neil Postman often asked, "What is the problem to which this is the solution?" If your innovation doesn't provide a solution to a significant problem, why waste your time innovating in that area? On the other hand, if your innovation solves an important problem, then you have some potent fuel for your own persistence and motivation.

Find and Generate New Ideas and Perspectives

Give yourself time to play, brainstorm, and generate possibilities, both alone and with others. I love to use the SCAMPER model. SCAMPER is an acronym for Substitute, Combine, Adapt, Modify, Put to another use, Eliminate, and Reverse. Google SCAMPER to find out more about this technique. I am also a fan of the book *ThinkerToys* by Michael Michalko, which gives multiple tips for brainstorming and creative thinking.

Beware of Confusing Scale with Innovation or the Entrepreneurial Spirit

While big gets more attention, if you have an innovation that addresses an important problem, don't worry about scale. If your idea helps a dozen people in great need, go for it. Of course, don't be naive about the fiscal realities. An institution is rarely going to make huge investments in an innovation that is small-scale but has a huge budget.

"Nail It Then Scale It"

In their book *Nail It Then Scale It*, Nathan Furr and Paul Ahlstrom suggest that entrepreneurs start small then scale up their innovations. If your goal is to scale something, start by doing what Jim Collins calls firing bullets before cannonballs. Test the idea, the need, and the market for your idea with smaller innovations. Once you build confidence and have some evidence that you're addressing a great need with a great solution that is in demand, then you can move to larger investments of time, energy, and money.

Innovate with Humility

Arrogance is not a prerequisite to innovation. You can innovate with humility, as I will explain further in a later chapter. Start by recognizing that you could be wrong, that you will and do make mistakes (sometimes big ones), and that there are often others who might be able to do the same work as well or better than you. I don't mean you should abandon your idea, but an attitude of humility does provide a healthy perspective.

On the night of his arrest, Jesus washed his disciples' feet. He explained that he was establishing a different model of leadership, one that sees itself as an opportunity to serve others, not to control them. I suggest pursuing educational innovation in the same spirit. Remember that educational innovation is best pursued with a noble cause, one that is more important than our individual reputations. Learning organizations driven by a cult of personality quickly become less about mission and more about amplifying the image of a person or group of people.

"If We Don't Do It, Who Will?"

My friend and mentor, Dr. Ross Stueber, once asked me this question when I was wondering if I was wasting my time on a project. His simple question put everything into perspective, and it gave me a way to focus my efforts.

Why not invest your life in the areas where others are less likely to act? Do what might not get done if you do not act. There are so many needs and problems in the education space. Some of those needs are attended to by hundreds or thousands of people and organizations, often because they are easy or offer great financial or other rewards. Why not invest in great needs that are off the radar of many others, needs that might not be met if we ignore them?

19

Tips for Promoting the Adoption of an Innovation

Given all this information, how do you progress toward the adoption of an innovation? Here are some practical ideas that can help.

Increase Awareness of the Possibilities

A simple way to increase others' awareness is through some strategic field trips. Consider identifying innovators and early adopters, and invite them to go with you to another learning organization where the innovation you want to promote has already been adopted. Whether it is an educational technology, a teaching method, or an overall school design, people need to be informed about the possibilities.

Notice that I suggested starting with innovators and early adopters. Invite others too early in the process and they are likely to come back with a list of reasons why your organization should not make any changes. As adoption develops in your organization, you can identify good places for later adopters to visit as well, but don't make the mistake of assuming that an extreme case is the best place for a later adopter to start. Consider models where a late adopter can meet and learn from another late adopter in a different organization about how that person made the transition and is now a champion for the cause.

Nurture Shared Ownership from Key Leaders in the Organization

There are certainly instances of grassroots adoptions of innovations. Yet, in most organizations, if the leadership does not own it and value it, you will be fighting resistance every step of the way. Worse, you will most likely lack the resources to make it happen.

Quite often you will need to make a case for the innovation to the key leaders in your organization. You will need to garner the financial support you need to move it forward, and ask those leaders to speak in favor of and even shift their priorities to bring about the innovation you're promoting. Even if it takes months or years, this can be a very good investment of your time and energy.

It is hard to overemphasize this part of the adoption process. If you are a school leader, then making sure your board is in agreement, even enthusiastic agreement, is often critical. If you are a teacher, make sure you nurture support from the principal or other key leaders in your school. You will need to have lots of conversations. In the process, be sure to listen for their interests, goals, and concerns. Only in this way can you help them to see the benefits of this innovation and how it will align with and support their goals.

One-on-One Conversations

Take the time to build relationships with others in the organization, and talk to people individually about the ideas and possibilities. You will be amazed at what will come from simply investing the time in these individual chats. I find that chats over coffee or lunch are extremely valuable.

Ask People for Help

There is something about helping another person that builds a connection and sense of commitment. Ask colleagues to help you as you begin to progress toward the adoption of the innovation you're advocating. Maybe they help you with a presentation you give. Maybe they create materials or resources. Maybe they provide candid feedback and input. By inviting others into your work, you give them a chance to test new ideas and build comfort with them. Just make sure that you ask people to help with something that matters. People don't like to be patronized or have their time wasted.

Pilot and Pilot Some More

The word "pilot" can be your best friend. Identify teachers who would be open to piloting your innovation in some way in their classroom or in other ways amid their work at the learning organization. Invite their opinions and input along the way. This gives them a front row seat to exploring the innovation, providing them with the time to weigh their concerns with the possibilities and opportunities.

Provide Information

Before they will adopt an innovation, most people need to be informed, learn about the benefits and drawbacks, and have a chance to explore and experiment. Start with providing non-threatening opportunities for people to dip their toes in the water. Create one-page handouts, a simple and easy website or blog, or offer a lunchtime tutorial or presentation. Find other ways to help people get the necessary information and to learn more about the innovation. Answer common questions. Inform. Don't be afraid to persuade. Consider using resources like Howard Gardner's seven levers for changing minds or Robert Cialdini's six principles of persuasion.

Show and Tell

As some teachers start to adopt the innovation, coordinate opportunities for other teachers to visit and see the innovation in action. Remember that the late adopters will not be readily convinced by the innovators. Late adopters need to see late majority and/or early majority people adopting and using the innovation before they can consider being open to it. (There is a more detailed discussion of how people adopt innovation in the earlier chapter entitled "Understanding the Adopters of Educational Innovation.")

Bring in an Expert

It can be helpful to invite leading experts into the community to show and teach what they know about the innovation. For some in the community, this added expert opinion will offer a little more credibility to the innovation. However, remember that people tend to be most influenced by people with whom they share similar concerns and interests. So, if the expert is seen as an innovator or is viewed as being disconnected from the real world of their learning organization, some may find it hard to listen and accept such expert input.

Provide Simulated Experiences

Many people will not try something new in a real classroom or context until they've had ample time to test it in a safer, low-risk context. Set up some of those models and provide support for people to try out the innovation. Look for low risk and low barriers to entry.

Celebrate Successes

As new people adopt the innovation and have good experiences with it, capture those experiences and share them with others in the community. Celebrate what is going well. This might be a simple email, a gathering over dessert or a meal, creating visuals in the hallways, or any other creative idea. The important part is that you are celebrating success and people are seeing that.

Debrief Setbacks

Things will not always go well. Innovations can have glitches and exceptions that become fuel for resistance. Don't let rumors about those setbacks spread in the community. Find out what happened, why it happened, and figure out how to fix or prevent it the next time. Help people to work through the difficulties and turn them into success stories. Then share those stories.

Some disagree with me on this, but I believe that it builds important credibility for you to be the first to know and highlight the problems, limitations, and setbacks of an innovation. Do you really want to be someone who pushes for an innovation that is not good or truly beneficial? Do your homework. Bring problems to the surface. Explore the glitches together, and work to solve them or manage them. If it isn't a good innovation, be willing to kill it. In the long run, this is better for you and for the organization. This is a key to creating an authentic culture.

Devise Team Workshops

"Sit and get" in-service trainings are of limited value. However, all that changes in a workshop setting where you place people in intentionally organized groups based on your best guess at where they fit as adopters. In the workshop, have people plan and create something related to the innovation. Such a setting is a chance for some positive peer support and influence. Think practical and hands-on, and try to include mechanisms so that people can try out and learn to use what they build.

The Mandate

Sometimes, a mandate will work. If leadership is on board and your innovation is seen as mission critical, it could be time to work with the leadership to communicate a reasonable but clear organizational goal or direction for the community. If you are that leadership, and you have a sense that now is the time, just do it, but if you do, be sure that you are ready to give the time and resources necessary so that people can make the transition.

Before you begin, gauge your community. Some communities will approach such a mandate with bitterness, holding a grudge and waiting for the whole thing to fail. Others respond favorably because there is a measure of trust and the culture has tolerance for some strong central leadership decisions.

Team Scouts

Identify a group of trusted and respected members in the community and ask them to review a given innovation and make recommendations about if and how to adopt it. Give them the time and resources for a thorough analysis (classes, readings, connections with experts, visits to and interviews with others who have adopted it, and so on.). Make this a dream team and then support their decisions when they report back. At the beginning, provide clear questions and direction for the group, and then work closely with them to help act on what they find and recommend.

Invest in Internal Experts

If you find some innovators and early adopters who want to champion the innovation, invest in them. Provide them with the support and resources to become world-class with the innovation. Then promote their work more broadly: in the local media, at conferences, through various external venues. Celebrate their success and influence within the community. Their thought leadership can be a powerful force. It can also help associate your school's identity in the public's mind with the innovation.

Highlight the Problems

Be careful not to be manipulative with this one, but innovations should be about addressing key problems or taking advantage of promising opportunities. Finding ways to discover and highlight problems that the innovation addresses is a great way to build a case for it. After all, innovations are about solving problems and pursuing opportunities.

There are countless other elements to the adoption of an innovation in your learning organization, but the ideas in this essay can be a helpful starting point. Don't treat them like a recipe, but rather, see them as suggestions. Consider becoming more familiar with the diffusion of innovation research, as that is a helpful tool for understanding the dynamics at work when an innovation is introduced to a community. From there, you can use these suggestions, along with other ideas, to work toward a culture that embraces something new for the benefit of learners.

20

Strategies for Promoting Social Innovation and Entrepreneurship in Your Learning Organization

Imagine how the world would change if learning organizations around the globe started to nurture thought- and practice-related innovation and social entrepreneurship.

In *Creating Innovators*, author Tony Wagner proposed seven survival skills he says we should emphasize in our learning organizations. Those skills include "critical thinking and problem solving, collaboration across networks and leading by influence, agility and adaptability, initiative and entrepreneurship, effective oral and written communication, accessing and analyzing information, along with curiosity and imagination."

Few of these skills typically show up as distinct titles in schools' catalogs of class offerings, but it doesn't take much convincing to recognize that these are valuable traits in the contemporary world, traits that would serve a person well in becoming an active citizen and developing a high level of human agency and self-direction. A person who has these traits is not only more employable, offering more value in the workplace, but is also more able to benefit others and effect positive change in the world.

Toward Learning Organizations that Make a Difference

What if learning organizations focused less on tests and homework and more on empowering difference-making and positive change?

Are you ready to get started? If so, here are some ideas. Most of them are simple projects and strategies that any willing school (K-12 or university) could add. I eliminated from this list projects that require larger financial investments, suggesting instead strategies that most learning organizations could launch in the next month to a year.

The President's (or Principal's) Challenge

Every year, Harvard's president identifies a global or social challenge and invites groups of students across the campus to engage in entrepreneurial efforts to address that challenge throughout the year. There is a launch event, mentors who work with interested students, set times to share and celebrate the students' work, and an annual winner. Similar projects could be replicated in elementary schools, high schools, flagship state students, or smaller liberal arts colleges. While it's true that many schools don't have a fully staffed innovation center for coordinating such a project, any school can improvise on this basic plan.

Missions over Majors

Sarah Stein Greenberg cast a vision for a future university in which students would declare missions to solve problems in the world instead of declaring traditional majors. Greenberg's vision requires a major shift in thinking about higher education, but until that shift occurs, we can still devise projects within the spirit of the idea. Colleges could allow students to declare a mission instead of a minor, allowing them to create a personalized learning plan that helps them to pursue that mission. Or maybe students or groups of students in K-12 education could have an annual challenge to identify personally meaningful missions that they would then pursue throughout the school year, keeping a portfolio of their learning and progress. Their work could even be included as a "course" on their transcript.

Tell the Stories

There are so many amazing stories to tell about social entrepreneurship, so many innovations that contribute to society. Learn about those stories and invite the people involved in them into your school to share their stories with the students. If being there in person is not possible, then bring those people into your school via Skype or Google Hangouts. Make your school a place where social-impact storytelling ignites the passions and interests of young people.

Give Students Compelling Answers When They Ask Why

When K-12 students ask, "Why do we need to learn this?" frame answers around how knowledge and skill in each discipline can benefit society. How have people in the past used math, history, or biology to benefit the world? How can our knowledge and skill help? Answers that are more about society than about schooling will be of more benefit to students who have heretofore been told that they should learn math, for instance, so they can be ready for the math in college. A better answer might be that we learn math so that we can use mathematical thinking to solve real and important problems in our lives, in the workplace, and in the world. Give examples, and challenge students to come up with more examples.

Create Dedicated Community-Based Learning Courses

I first learned about community-based learning courses at a conference presentation several years ago from someone at Dominican University. Faculty members identify certain sections of a course as a community-based learning course. It has the same course-level outcomes as other sections of the same course, but this designation means that part of the learning will take place in and through community-based service learning. In other words, the student can take art, psychology, history, or science classes that not only teach them about those subjects, but they do so, in part, by using that budding knowledge to help with a community issue. Students can opt to sign up either for the community-based course or a more traditional version of the course.

Turn a Course Project into an Engine for Addressing Social Needs

Maybe your school isn't ready to create full community-based learning courses, but any school could apply the concept on the assignment level. Create an assignment in a class where students propose or seek to create proposed solutions to real-world social issues. You could even launch the event with a quick field trip to see the problem in person, or ask a community representative come into the classroom and explain the problem. Help students learn how to ask good questions, research, and investigate, and then use what they learn in the class to solve the problem.

Use Case Studies and/or CaseQuests

Challenge students to use their knowledge in a subject by analyzing real-world case studies. This helps them to see the relevance of what they are learning, while also helping them learn to apply that knowledge in contexts they are likely to experience beyond the classroom. All students, whether in kindergarten or graduate school, can benefit from this method. (Find out more about CaseQuests, which provides case studies online for business students, at www.casequest.net.)

Internships and Shadowing

Many colleges and universities offer opportunities for students to shadow professionals or participate in internships, but this concept could have even broader applications. Why not make an effort to build partnerships and create opportunities with groups and people working on social issues in the world, whether they are nonprofit entities or for-profit businesses with a beneficent mindset?

Teach Social Entrepreneurship Skills

Offer an elective course on social entrepreneurship for interested students, or even make a commitment to teach about social entrepreneurship and related skills across a major or throughout the curriculum.

Build Connections with Outside Groups

A growing number of events and groups are dedicated to social entrepreneurship. Connect with them and learn from them. Participate in social entrepreneurship challenges that are open to the public and to schools. Connect with groups like the Social Venture Network, Changemakers®, the Social Enterprise Alliance, the Social Enterprise Association (which is focused on Singapore but is still a great resource), or the countless social entrepreneurship groups, programs, and efforts in colleges and universities.

You don't need to reinvent the wheel when it comes to social entrepreneurship; build on the work of those who have gone before you. Network, collaborate, and build meaningful connections with other groups that might have people or resources that can help your local efforts.

21

How to Maximize the Effect of an Edupreneur in Your Learning Organization

There is a good chance that you have at least a couple of edupreneurs in your school, that is, educators with an entrepreneurial flair. If you want them to stick around, make sure you're helping them to have a powerful effect on the students, the school, the community, and the world.

Edupreneurs are the sometimes eccentric but always passionate and driven teachers who want to create, innovate, and conjure the spirit of a startup in education. Often an edupreneur is called forth when a teacher identifies a problem, need, or opportunity and feels compelled to do something about it. Edupreneurs are action-oriented; they want to see tangible results. Does this sound like the type of educator who might have something to offer to your school and your students? Is this the type of person that you might want to keep around? If so, here are some tips for doing just that.

Differentiate

We get the idea of having differentiated instruction for students. How about differentiating for teachers, staff, and administrators? Doing the same thing for every person is sometimes the least fair way of going about things. At the very least, it is a certain way to ensure that you don't help everyone to perform at their maximum capacity. Instead of treating every teacher the same, consider what each teacher and staff member needs, not only to survive the day, but to thrive. Make it your goal to offer differentiated leadership.

Leave Space for Innovation

Sometimes school leaders establish policies and procedures that verge on micromanagement. While some employees thrive in that kind of environment, wanting detailed and prescribed activities, many others do not, and this is especially so for edupreneurs. Edupreneurs need room to experiment, explore, and innovate, and that means finding ways to loosen up on the reins a bit. In fact, there may even be times when you want to give them the freedom and flexibility to work beyond the standard policies and procedures so they can launch something new. Just be aware that allowing your edupreneurs more freedom will have an effect on the overall culture of your organization, and be prepared to manage perceptions.

Affirm the Innovators

Find ways to affirm the innovative work of the edupreneurs. Make sure they know that you value their contributions and appreciate their distinct gifts and abilities. Keep in mind that different people appreciate different forms of affirmation. Some might be honored by a public recognition of their work while others might be humiliated or annoyed by it. This means taking the time to affirm them, but also learning the forms of affirmation that will truly lift up that person.

Help Them Find the Time and Resources

Innovation takes both time and resources. When possible and proper, look for creative ways to give them the time they need as well as a bit of financial support to work on a new project. If that means calling an innovative idea a pilot and making them the official lead for it, then give that a try.

Redefine Failure

An edupreneur won't thrive in a highly risk-averse context. If you want to reap the benefits of having such people in your school, then you'll need to learn to celebrate failures as learning experiences and stepping-stones toward future endeavors. Of course, you'll want to manage the risk and make sure other organizational priorities aren't compromised in the process, but if you have those things in check, give edupreneurs room to fail and don't treat their failures like character flaws. Aim for a goal of positive effect more than polished perfectionism.

Value the Lopsided Edupreneur

I mentioned earlier in this book that some of the most innovative and entrepreneurial people are wonderfully lopsided. In other words, they don't necessarily have a perfectly balanced set of skills, knowledge, and abilities. However, they likely have a few amazing and well-refined skills and abilities that allow them to make an enormous difference.

Help wonderfully lopsided people to work on areas where they need to grow, to iron out those quirks and characteristics that could hurt them or others or keep them from being successful. At the same time, it is equally important—maybe even more important—to encourage them to build on their strengths. In other words, if they excel in one area, don't think that the goal is to then help them to excel in an area where they are weak. Instead, think about how you can help them build on their strengths.

Be Open to New Titles, Structures, and Processes

Innovation is, by nature, about doing things that are not being done. Since that's the case, it is unlikely that there is a set of policies, rules, and job descriptions that fits what an edupreneur might be trying to do. Be open to creating new positions, new job descriptions, and new structures that give them what they need to flourish.

Trust Them but Stay True to Your Convictions

You are not going to see or understand everything edupreneurs are trying or thinking. Some of their ideas may even seem downright silly. You will need to find a balance between trusting them to innovate when you don't understand everything about what they're up to and staying true to your values and convictions for the school. Make your expectations clear, but also be willing to give them the freedom to do things that you don't yet understand.

Keep Putting the Students First

These innovators have wonderful gifts to offer, but your first priority is to the well-being and education of the students. In the frenzy of creating and innovating, some edupreneurs may occasionally lose sight of certain critical elements. They may be willing to take risks that you are not willing to take, not when other key priorities are at stake. With that in mind, you can support them, but do so within the boundaries that you consider important, and communicate those boundaries clearly, explaining why they are important to you. Sometimes you will set boundaries in the wrong place, so be humble enough to see that and change. Other times, the edupreneur may decide that she needs more freedom and flexibility than is possible in your school. That is okay.

Let Them Go

Some edupreneurs will be delighted to spend a long career in your school, but that is not necessarily the calling for all of them. Some will benefit your school, develop new skills while there, and then be called to something else. Accept that. Don't try to guilt them into staying. Make sure they know that they are valued and supported as long as they want to stay, but also be the first to give them your blessing and support as they go to start the next big education business, open a new school, or apply their gifts in a new context.

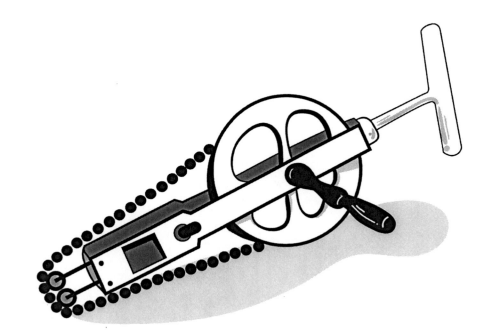

22

Use At Your Own Risk:
Metaphors and Illustrations for Educational Change

Do you ever find yourself having to defend the importance of an educational innovation in your organization? Are you trying to spark some lively discussions about what needs to change in your learning organization?

Skeptics argue that things are working fine now. "Why change?" they ask. Or they point to the metaphorical garbage dump of educational trends and innovations that failed to deliver in the past. While skeptics may well have good and valid points to discuss, explore, and consider, many of us find ourselves speaking to people in groups both large and small, trying to articulate why we consider it important to innovate, and why it is important for people in our learning organizations to think about what might need to change.

If this is your struggle, then I've put together a collection of quotes, analogies, and metaphors that you can use to get the discussion started. Use them at your own risk.

"He who rejects change is the architect of decay. The only human institution which rejects progress is the cemetery."—Harold Wilson

This quotation speaks for itself. While we do not promote change for the sake of change, living and vibrant institutions do change, adapt, and respond to the world around them, and this quote can serve as a useful discussion starter. Are we changing? How? Is it for the better? How can we promote positive and needed change?

Educational Malpractice

At a distance learning conference a few years ago, Chris Dede argued that the time is coming when failing to use the current and best teaching and learning technologies will be a form of educational malpractice. Just as a medical professional who insists on using outdated technologies when more effective ones at his or her disposal can be faulted, so can educators. If technologies are tools (I'm not especially fond of this metaphor, but I'll go with it for now), then it is important to use the best and most proper tool for the job. Would you go to a brain surgeon who insisted on using an 18th century skull saw? What is the equivalent in our education system today?

I fully support respecting and valuing diverse perspectives, but there comes a time when we need to acknowledge some limits, such as when we are sitting in a surgeon's (or teacher's) office and she is preaching to us about the superiority of the time-tested skull saw over these new technological trends. We can appreciate this person's nostalgia for the "good old days" while respectfully insisting that we put the well-being of the patient—or the learner—ahead of our own comfort and preferences.

The Mr. Potato Head Analogy

The original Mr. Potato Head was a potato with some pushpins. Over time, the lowly potato became regulated into the mass produced, standardized, plastic product we see on store shelves today.

Education suffers a similar fate sometimes. We formalize, add policy after policy, and eventually have something safe and sterile that's not at all the same as our original goal or vision. As we go about making small adjustments and gradual changes, we need to challenge the entire system occasionally to ask if we have sanitized and sterilized the system so much that we have strayed from our core mission. If we find that we have, how can we address the current state of affairs?

"We're Not in Kansas Anymore"

When Dorothy arrives in Oz, she looks around and then says to her dog, "Toto, I've a feeling we're not in Kansas anymore." Then the Good Witch of the North comes down from the sky and Dorothy quips, "Now I know we're not in Kansas."

These quotes from the memorable scene in the classic film make a good introduction for talking about what has changed in the world over the past decade and how schools need to respond to our changing world. We are not in Kansas anymore and our students don't live in a Kansas-like world. How do we best prepare them for life in the world as it now is and as it hurtles into the future?

The Post-Factory School

This metaphor is sometimes overused, but it serves a useful role in conversations with many educators. As some are quick to note, much of the modern schooling model comes from an industrial age that sought to prepare people for industrial work. The school model included bells, rows, and a grading system similar to that used in the rating of different meats and other products.

However, we live in a post-industrial age, which calls for new knowledge, skills, and abilities—and a different type of school system. This notion can be a helpful discussion starter as we consider the future of formal education. How is our school like a factory? What would it take to make it a post-factory school?

Fishing Lessons or a Fish Distribution Center?

Another way to illustrate the change that we want to promote in our learning organizations is to contrast a fish distribution center with the example of a father teaching his son to fish.

The first example is of a place where people can go to buy or receive fish that were caught and cleaned by others. A fish distribution center is easier, perhaps more convenient, and it requires less from the recipient.

The example of fishing lessons illustrates a qualitatively different experience. The father nurtures the boy and teaches him the details and skills needed to fish so that eventually the boy can catch, clean, and eat as many fish as he wants. He can even pass on this skill to others.

To apply this metaphor to schools, the first model leaves the person continually dependent upon others to teach them. The second example seeks to help each learner become self-directed, eventually becoming a self-teacher and a self-learner. The model of the son learning how to fish represents the type of change and innovation that we want to promote in our schools. Traditional teacher-directed models risk failing to meet such a goal. What would it take for your school to shift from a fish distribution center to a place where fishing is learned? What would that look like?

The Remote Control

Imagine that you are listening to me give a presentation and you start to get bored. You then notice a remote control. Out of curiosity, you pick it up. In a playful moment, you press the pause button, and to your amazement, I pause. Recognizing the power in your hands, you experiment with the other features on the remote. You fast-forward me, rewind, stop, and even try the picture-in-picture feature so that you can watch your favorite team play in the corner while I present. Then you click the record button. When you get home at night, you find that you can replay parts of my presentation that interested you and skip over the ones that do not.

Now imagine a learning environment where such an experience was possible. What would be the benefits and drawbacks of that? Now consider that we have all the tools and technologies right now to do this very thing. Consider the possibilities! How can we empower each learner with his or her own personal remote control?

Students as the Audience—or as Actors, Directors, and Playwrights

How will students ever develop the skills we say we want for them—to perform, lead others, create, and design—if in their schooling all they ever do is play the role of the audience? When can we give them the chance to practice performing, being leaders, creating and designing, and developing competence and confidence in these other roles? What educational changes or innovations can we make to help students progress toward these powerful roles?

Load-Bearing Walls

In *Inevitable: Mass Customized Learning: Learning in an Age of Empowerment* by Charles Schwahn and Beatrice McGarvey, the authors use a metaphor of load-bearing walls to understand the challenges of change in a schooling model. Load-bearing walls bear the weight of a structure and keep the roof of a building from falling. Similarly, we build our schools upon certain ideas and practices that become integral to the overall school structure. Careless changing of these elements can cause the school to crumble figuratively.

If we want to make a change to one of these integral components—as we would if we were making changes to a load-bearing wall in a building—we need to add reinforcements and have a clear plan on how we will ensure that the structure will remain sound. We might even need to add new and improved load-bearing walls.

This metaphor can be a great discussion starter about what we consider to be the load-bearing walls in our organizations and what sort of remodeling is in order. First, we will need to ask why this remodel is worthwhile. Is it worth the risk? How are we going to make sure the integrity of the system is maintained while we make the changes?

The authors argue that the load-bearing walls in most schools are grade levels, students assigned to classrooms, bell schedules, courses, textbooks, a traditional letter-grade system, report cards, and a nine-month school year. If you plan to replace one or more of these components, make sure that you plan carefully.

Giant Slaying

While this metaphor might be a bit violent for some people's taste, its comparison to education is growing on me. It is a rooted in a question that challenges us to think about the types of experiences that we are giving young people as they grow and learn: How are we helping students grow into dragon or giant slayers, in the figurative sense, of course?

Our students are people with courage, skill, character, and conviction. Is sitting in a desk in straight rows really what they need? I like to think of the story of young David defeating the giant Goliath with a sling. How did David prepare for that? Did he get an "A" in giant slaying 101 in school? No. He tended sheep. As he did that work, he had to protect the sheep from lions and other predators. He probably spent hours practicing with that sling while passing the time as a shepherd boy. Of course, according to the biblical account, he also had a little divine assistance.

What are the parallels in the story of David and Goliath with how young people learn today? Are they getting the opportunities they need to gain the confidence and skill to take on and defeat the figurative giants that they will face in their lives? If not, what do we need to change to help them? What sort of learning organization nurtures people such as these? The group might want to list off some figurative giants that young people are likely to face in their lives, and then think about how to give them the experiences they need to prepare for their lives to come.

Section IV:
Knowing and Nurturing Your
Personal Practices and Perspectives

23

Staying Current and Educational Innovation as a Calling

"How do you stay current in your field, and how do you find the time to do what you do?" I often hear these questions when I am chatting with people after a speaking engagement.

Part of the answer to these questions is that I consider it my job, even my calling, to stay current. Only in this way can I can analyze the trends, consider the benefits and drawbacks, and synthesize what I learn so that it is useful for others and for my own educational projects, and only in this way can that knowledge become a creative spark for new possibilities. Staying current takes time, lots of it, so I will not offer any quick tips or claims that Twitter or some other social media will provide the answers.

Instead, here is a list of some things that I do. These are not rules or even guidelines for myself. They simply describe how I tend to think and act. I don't suggest that these are the right actions for anyone else, but they give a bit more insight into how I go about much of my own life's work and calling. Perhaps you will find some ideas or tips that help in your own self-designed strategy for staying current.

Minimize Consumption of Television and Other Entertainment Media

I watch my share of movies and television shows but most often not daily. In fact, I sometimes go weeks without watching a single movie or television show, especially when I am in the middle of following some new intellectual lead. However, I have my down times, times when I take a break from my standard reading and studying. During those periods, which can range from a few hours to several weeks, I might watch quite a bit of television and see a few movies. There have even been periods of two to three months where I set aside my regular schedule of reading and studying. I just see that as a natural cycle. Of course, I don't spend months on end watching television or movies endlessly, but I might watch a great deal more than normal during my down times and spend more time taking it easy.

Consider What I Do to Be a Lifestyle and a Calling

Studying and analyzing the trends in educational innovation is not simply a part of my daytime job. It is something that I pursue at night, on weekends, and during lunch as well. I strive to devote quality time to my family, too, but I find that there are plenty of time slots, for instance from about nine in the evening to one in the morning, when I can be very productive in my study and research. On weekends in our family, there are hours where everyone decides to do something on their own, when my wife will be reading or exercising, for instance, and the kids will play with each other, and those times, too, can be productive ones for me. A typical week of research and exploring occupies twenty or thirty hours beyond my regular hours at work. These hours do not feel like work for me. What I do in those hours is part of my calling, and that makes them tremendously meaningful and satisfying for me. As I see it, my research and study are as much a part of my identity as the lifestyle commitment that might come with being a professional athlete (not that I'm claiming an equivalent talent).

Continue to Build a Personal Learning Network

There is plenty of literature about building personal learning networks. How I go about it is that I follow interesting and leading thinkers and doers on Twitter; I subscribe to multiple blogs; I sign up for newsletters from certain excellent sources; I network through my own blog; I read book reviews; I attend conferences and events, both physical and virtual; and I participate in any number of online groups.

Go to the Primary Sources

Many people in education get most of their ideas from secondary sources such as textbooks and people who aggregate, synthesize, or share packaged versions of an idea. I read those, but I often use them to track down the original sources, too. I find the scholarly journal articles and books, and I sometimes reach out to interview the people behind the ideas. I also try to visit some learning organizations in person so that I can see the ideas in action by the people who are leading the way. In this way I learn from all sorts of fascinating organizations, and I hope to learn from even more education startups in the future, as going to the source makes an enormous difference in my work. It is one thing to be aware of or informed about something like self-directed learning. It is quite another to connect with and learn directly from some of the leaders in that area.

By the way, when I think of the leaders of a certain trend or innovation, I do not necessarily mean the person with the most popular blog, the viral YouTube video, the elite university credentials, or the most impressive title. By "leader" I mean the person who is doing the critical thinking and work behind the idea. Today, that is often not the most recognized name in the area or even the person publishing in the scholarly journals on the subject. It takes work and skill to identify these people, but it is worth the time and effort. This differentiates my working and thinking from the rest of the crowd.

Read the Hard and Boring Stuff

Reading the hard and boring stuff goes hand-in-hand with tracking down the primary sources, and it is equally critical. Tracking something back to its source might mean that you read a five-hundred-page text that makes only partial sense to you. You persist with it and try to glean as much as possible from it. It is okay to understand only ten percent of an enormously complex text the first time around.

At times, reading such a text will be like sitting in a room of people who are conversing in a language you don't understand. You could leave the room, ignore what's going on around you, or give your absolute attention to the conversation, attending to every word you can catch and paying attention to body language so that you can walk away with at least a drop of meaning. While you might not understand much of what you hear, if you attend to the conversation in the latter way, you will get more out of it than you would if you leave the room or ignore the people around you.

I think of difficult books and readings in this way, and usually, when I do, the difficult gets a bit easier. Even when it doesn't, I find I learn more when I persist in reading the "hard stuff" than I do when I try to understand a trend, model, or innovation only through popular and secondary sources.

Surf

I'm not speaking here of surfing the web, but of using a focused transmedia approach. When I learn about a new term, person, model, or company, I often seek out more sources that will help me learn more about it. Such a search might take me to online content, an obscure book, another interview or conversation, a visit or a road trip, the old-fashioned library, or some form of digital media. From that source, I might learn about yet another idea, which I would then trace elsewhere. I am surfing from source to source in pursuit of a deeper understanding. While convenience might lead us to stick with only the Internet, some of my most rewarding experiences have come from tracking an idea across media and sources: from book to book, digital to analog, journal to film, blog post to email interaction, Tweet to face-to-face visit. I might surf through a single idea for months or even several years, usually surfing among multiple ideas and projects at a time.

Apply It

I have an applied focus in my work, as I am ultimately interested in doing things that matter. This perspective means that I do more than just read and talk about an idea. I put that idea into practice. I apply it, experiment with it, and innovate with it. If I want to know more about MOOCs, then sooner or later I am going to take one or a dozen; then I'll need to design one and teach one. The same thing goes for other alternate models of education, such as self-directed learning or project-based learning. It is very rare for me to study something without making it a part of who I am or what I do in some way. These direct experiences give me insights that I would never gain even from the best books.

Write and Talk About It

I think out loud or in text, so to process certain ideas, I need to have conversations about them or journal or blog about them. Or, as I am doing right now, I might write a book about them. In doing so, I am able to organize my thoughts, notice new connections, and discover more trains of thought.

Go to Idea-Rich Events

We all know that all conferences are not created equal. I try to find the idea events that are at the heart of what I am exploring. Then I attend, listen, learn, connect with others, and learn more about what I'm interested in.

In my research of leaders of innovative learning organizations, I have consistently found that these types of leaders do not only network with the people who are easily accessible to them by way of proximity or familiarity. They seek out connections with other innovators and thought leaders. They want to inspire and be inspired by the best ideas in the world, and that means that they look for the places where those ideas are shared and where people converse and connect around those ideas, places where the next great innovations begin. In education, that might be events like the *Education Innovation Summit*, SXSWEdu, some of the TEDx events, or a number of other niche events inside or outside the formal field of education.

Disconnect

I don't mean what I write here to be some sort of digital detox advertisement, but I do note that disconnecting is a critical part of the thinking and designing process. By "disconnect" in this context, I don't mean to suggest that I disconnect from all things digital, but I do disconnect from a design project, a line of inquiry, or a thought project from time to time.

It is not uncommon for me to read over a hundred books year, hundreds of journal articles, and lots of online content. To process, discover new connections, and let ideas begin to influence my plans and thinking, I find that I need to step away sometimes. I might exercise, take a nap, sit in the back yard, ignore the first suggestion on this list, try something new, play or listen to music, work on a puzzle with the kids, enjoy an extra-long lunch, or almost anything else as long as it is does not relate to my current project. Some of my most exciting ideas appear during those down times. When they do, I jot them down in my idea book and continue to enjoy my down time.

This is how I stay current and experiment with educational design and innovation. I genuinely consider what I do to be a calling, and I don't think of it as work. It is just who I am and what I do. I'm not sure that this would necessarily be of direct value to others, as it is really just the path that seems best for my calling. Other callings require different lifestyles. Nonetheless, I offer this in response to those who are curious enough to ask me the question, "How do you stay current and find the time to do what you do? Perhaps readers will find specific tips that will work for them along with a broader inspiration to map out their own strategies for staying current.

24

When It Comes to Educational Innovation, Are You a Tortoise or a Hare?

When most people remember Aesop's fable about the tortoise and the hare, they think of the tortoise winning the race because it was slow and steady all the way to the finish line. However, the hare's overconfidence did not give the tortoise enough of an edge so that it could win the race. The tortoise actually had to run that race. It had to stick its neck out and persevere despite huge odds against it. As James Bryant Conant is quoted as saying, "Behold the turtle. He makes progress only when he sticks his neck out."

Of course, there are other perspectives. Anita Brookner wrote, "In real life, it is the hare who wins. Every time. Look around you. And in any case it is my contention that Aesop was writing for the tortoise market. Hares have no time to read. They are too busy winning the game." In the fable, the hare's natural capacities gave it a huge advantage, if it were not for its character.

There are certainly hares at work in the field of educational innovation, those fast-moving innovators who experience early wins or achieve "firsts" in the field. However, sometimes those innovators find themselves so far ahead of the competition that their drive for innovation and new ventures diminishes, and they rest on their past accomplishments. Others don't have the resources to persist, while still others are quick off the blocks but don't have what it takes to make it all the way to the finish line.

Some argue that hares who are humble, determined, well resourced, and focused are likely to beat out the hard-working tortoise almost every time in the real world. Yet, that is often not what we see in educational innovation. I've been involved with plenty of "firsts" in the education sector, and those experiences provided me with a glimpse of what was possible. Pretty much every time, however, I did not have the human or other resources to amplify and refine the innovation. I gladly accepted my role and allowed other organizations to take the ideas, refine them, scale them, and monetize them. These other organizations were on the leading edge of those innovations, and it was their resources and capacity to execute and scale that gave them the advantage. They were really good at focusing, persisting, putting in the hard work and resources, and reaching the target audience.

Educational innovators who identify with the tortoise need to move beyond their safe and protected shells and take risks. But first, they have to agree to run the race in the first place. Perhaps we can think of the tortoises as the steady, persistent, determined, calculated risk-takers who are in it for the long haul. They don't resist change. They have the courage and confidence to get in the race in the first place. They recognize that the field of education is a dynamic, ever-changing endeavor. They may not move the fastest but they persist and keep their eyes on the goal.

While some still look at it as a competition, education is social entrepreneurship, and the end goal is for the best ideas to spread and have the greatest positive effect. That means that there is plenty of room and a valuable role for hares, tortoises, and any number of other participants. Whenever you can find that sweet spot that blends optimal capacity with optimal character, your chance of success is greatly improved.

25

Nurturing Personal Perspectives on Educational Change and Innovation

We are in an era of educational experimentation, and it is hard to argue against the fact that the digital revolution fuels much of this experimentation. Many aspects of traditional schooling are being questioned, some abandoned in search of new possibilities for student-centered, customized, high-impact learning experiences, all with the hope of equipping students for the unique challenges and opportunities of the contemporary world.

I am excited about this experimentation, and others are, too, but still others are skeptical, exhausted by the seemingly constant influx of educational trends. Just when you get comfortable with one, another arrives to replace it, they complain.

Wherever you find yourself on this spectrum of emotional or intellectual responses, it's pretty certain that educational systems will not return to the dominant models of the recent past. While educational experimentation had been waning over the past 70 years, such experimentation has always been with us, and today educational experimentation is becoming mainstream once more.

I offer here some perspectives that can offer insights on today's educational experimentation, insights that can help us to avoid marrying the spirit of the age, as William Inge warns us, and finding ourselves widowers in the future. As an educational leader, innovator, or entrepreneur, it is helpful to nurture each of these perspectives in yourself. They will help you to have a deeper and more nuanced approach to the many factors that affect innovation in education. I am certainly not trying to slow educational innovation with what I offer here, but I do hope that these insights can help us to shape the innovations that we choose to embrace, and perhaps even help us to decide which ones to embrace or inspire us to come up with innovations of our own.

The Historical Perspective

Looking at the history of education allows us to gain new insight into changes and innovations of the past. Things that we consider central attributes of schooling might turn out to be relatively new when we look at the broader historical perspective. For instance, grade-based classes, bells, and letter grades are relatively new. People still learned before letter grades and traditional schools existed. They are not the essence of an education.

Similarly, when we look at the history of education, we find that today's innovations are sometimes like models and methods of the past, but we also discover that certain aspects of contemporary education do not seem to have an historical equal. In addition, when we look at the history of change and innovation in the field of education, we learn more about why things changed. We may even discover that the changes we now embrace did not occur to improve student learning but instead may be innovations of necessity or efforts to increase scale or efficiency.

I am not referring to some broad introduction to the history of education here. I refer instead to historical thinking, asking specific questions and exploring what history can teach us about those questions: What is the history of letter grades and report cards? What is the history of distance education, including forms that existed before the Internet? What about the history of childhood? Has childhood always existed or is our contemporary notion more of a social construct? What about the history of grade-based learning, where students study alongside people of their own age? How old is that? What about the history of the book, and how did books change education? What other educational models existed in the past?

Asking historical questions gives us a depth of insight from which we can experiment or resist certain experiments today, but only if we do this questioning deeply and honestly. Such an inquiry is not about finding historical ammunition to win our personal educational battles. For this perspective to help us, we need to strive for insight, even if the insights challenge our positions or educational preferences.

The historical perspective is among the more overlooked and yet more powerful perspectives for educational innovators. The past is full of insights and inspiration for the current and aspiring educational innovator. If you have ever used a slingshot, you know that you have to pull back to gain momentum for launching something. A similar truth exists with educational innovation. Looking back can give us incredible insights and momentum to launch something new.

The Global Perspective

While some people have opportunities to experience different educational systems around the world, many do not. However, anyone can read about, network with, and visit educational systems around the world to gain rich insights into diverse educational models, metaphors, and methods. Striving to understand different perspectives offers a renewed appreciation for some of our own educational traditions as well as those from other parts of the world. We can ask what "education" and "learning" look like in areas that are distant from our own. Looking beyond school buildings, we gain new insights into the role of family, community, geography, and culture in education.

The Ethnographic Perspective

Ethnography is a research method that studies cultures, communities, and groups of people. The study of cultural artifacts, interviews, and lots of observation, even participant observation, all contribute to this method.

Ethnographic research is experiential. The researcher collects data with his or her own senses, testing those perceptions whenever possible. The ethnographic approach to studying education requires that we get out and do some interviewing and observing, asking ourselves and others those questions that will lead us to a deeper understanding of multiple types of learning communities.

Ethnography is the approach I use for studying innovative schools, and I can personally attest to the joy of learning that is possible through these experiences. It is a great way to get informed about the diverse models of education at work today. Charter schools are a great place to start, given that many of them have clear and distinct differences from other schools, such as project-based learning or game-based learning. Of course, not all of us have the time and resources to visit these schools in person, but the digital world gives almost all of us remote access to these people and places. Simply browsing YouTube videos and schools' websites can give us a taste of an ethnographic learning experience.

The Autobiographical Perspective

Each of us has a learning history that started with our conception, and exploring that history will help us to better understand our own beliefs, biases, values, and perspectives. Exploring educational change and innovation in view of our own learning histories allows us to gain new perspective on some of our moral, emotional, and intellectual reactions to the changes around us.

Such an exploration can show us that we do not always need to change our beliefs or values when change rolls around. This perspective can ground us and give us a sense of where we will and will not budge.

The Scientific Perspective

The educational possibilities that emerge from recent developments in brain research, positive psychology, organizational psychology, and the sociology of education are exciting. New findings in these areas give us an opportunity to examine and reexamine schools and education with fresh understanding.

The scientific perspective invites us to ask new questions. To what extent do our current systems, structures, and methods align with what we know about how people learn? How can we design schools and learning organizations that respect and/or maximize the design features of our brains and bodies? How can we cultivate positive strength-based learning communities? How can we use current research in psychology and sociology to create safe schools?

Of course, it is important to remember that research findings are tentative, and premature efforts to apply scientific findings to educational design are dangerous and misplaced. At the same time, ignoring the blessings of such research is equally mistaken. That is where comparing and contrasting scientific findings has value in shaping educational innovation. This is no easy task, but the scientific perspective is inadequate on its own.

The Philosophical Perspective

Questions about ethics, truth, and the nature of reality may seem esoteric, but they matter when it comes to education, as they do with pretty much all of life. Ignoring the philosophies that inform the many methods and models at work in education does not reduce their influence. However, ignoring them does risk minimizing both our influence and our understanding of why things happen the way they do.

The philosophical lens helps us to develop an understanding of things like homeschooling, religious education, Montessori schools, Waldorf schools, direct instruction, differentiated instruction, the concept of the community public school, the classical education movement, the open learning movement, distance education, and much more. There are philosophies at work in each of these, and simply analyzing educational movements by the sum of their observable parts would leave us with a flawed and incomplete understanding. Like it or not, we can't avoid exploring the philosophical side of things. However, just as with the historical perspective, it is easy to abuse this perspective, philosophizing so as to prove our pre-existing positions or educational ideologies. Instead, consider the benefits of using this perspective in the genuine pursuit of truth.

For those of you who come from a faith tradition (I, for example, am deeply proud of the Lutheran distinctions that inform my educational thought), I am including a theological perspective in the category of philosophical perspective, although I appreciate the argument that a separate theological perspective could be an appropriate and worthwhile addition to this list.

I'm sure there are many more perspectives that could benefit our experimentation and discourse about education today, but these are a good start, and I contend that many are critical to pursuing educational innovation of substance and long-term significance. In an age of for-profit education, edtech startups, constant innovation, and unprecedented educational experimentation, the field of education desperately needs innovators and leaders who are more than technicians. We need thinkers and designers who embrace the importance of viewing education through various lenses, including these six perspectives.

26

The Value of Newbies and Naysayers

I'll admit it. I can be a snob about some things. That is why I need daily reminders that the novice perspective can sometimes lead to greater innovation than that of person who has years of experience in a domain.

For example, I've been exploring the affordances and limitations of online learning since the 1990s, so when I read a news article in 2015 about this "new" development called online learning, I get frustrated. Or when people write about MOOCs as if they are the birth of online learning, I become suspicious about the veracity of their "research." I get irritated when people miss the fact that distance learning is centuries old, that online learning is decades old, and that there is a substantive body of research about both. That is why it is humbling but important for me to remind myself that we really need the newcomers and what might seem like "the uninformed" to imagine the future of blended and online learning.

I've had a certain conversation with more than 100 people over the years, people who are new to online learning, whether as a student, a teacher, or in some related role. The person will bring up a criticism about online learning that I might have settled in my mind a decade ago, but what they say reminds me that this concern is not settled for them. It isn't enough for me to say, "Well, that is a great question, but we've already looked at that and it isn't an issue." Of course it is an issue. If more than 100 people bring it up, it doesn't matter how much I want them to think or feel differently. If it's a concern to that many people, it's still worthy of consideration.

Another recurring conversation has to do with the use of live video in online courses. Numerous new faculty or students will tell me that their online courses would feel more personal if only the course could include more live video interactions. Countless people have told me that they think online learning will take off once video conferencing technology reaches a certain level of quality.

When I hear such comments, I'm tempted to point out that there are completely different paradigms for looking at the design of online learning that make little to no use of streaming video. If only they would read the great research, I think, about the promise and value of threaded discussions, asynchronous online collaboration tools, and dozens of online teaching strategies that produce exceptional results with helping students learn as much—and sometimes more—than they might have in a traditional face-to-face course. I can look at the sheer number of comments I read about how streaming video would make online learning better and more personal, and chalk it up to mass ignorance and people being uninformed about the research. Or I can get really curious about this trend.

Why do so many people keep coming back to this line of thinking? What is it about streaming video that attracts the attention of so many people? Maybe the perceived benefit isn't just that people want to apply a face-to-face teaching mindset to the online space. Maybe there is more to it than that, something that truly does have the potential to amplify both formal and informal online learning. Maybe streaming video in online classes would lead to greater adoption and engagement, because it's true that perceptions can influence reality for the online teacher as well as the learner.

I have learned so much from so-called novices and online learning newbies, and I've learned just as much from critics, people who view blended and online learning with lenses that are not standard to me. They see what I miss. They feel what I don't. They ask questions that I rarely or never considered. They propose solutions that sometimes seem absurd to me, but when they try those solutions, they actually work sometimes.

That is why I believe that students and teachers new to online learning, curious outside observers, and entrepreneurs with no background in the field may well be the future of the field. The same is true for many educational practices and innovations. Some of the most promising and disruptive ideas could come from these groups. Such people don't self-censor their way to inactivity. They are not simply building incremental changes based on past research and practice, because they know very little about those things. They have the advantage of looking at the field with a fresh perspective, uninformed by the educational ruts of past practice and dominant policy. The humility to listen and learn from these people, to partner with them, to invite their candid input and critiques may well be the source of the next great developments of education in a connected world.

27

Orbiting Academic Hairballs

In *Orbiting the Giant Hairball: A Corporate Fool's Guide to Surviving with Grace*, author Gordon MacKenzie writes that a hairball is "policy, procedure, conformity, compliance, rigidity, and submission to the status quo, while orbiting is originality, rules-breaking, non-conformity, experimentation, and innovation." His book focuses on how people in a corporate culture can maintain creativity and originality, but I could not help but think about how his ideas apply to those of us who seek out these same "orbiting" traits in schools and other learning organizations.

Some honor their creativity and originality by branching out on their own. They abandon the organization and venture into the world of consulting, freelancing, or startups. That is an admirable option, and I'm grateful for the amazing work that comes from people who choose this option. However, what intrigues me about MacKenzie's book is that he offers another option as well, an option he calls "orbiting the giant hairball." Here is how he explains it:

Orbiting is responsible creativity, vigorously exploring and operating beyond the hairball of the corporate mindset, beyond "accepted models, patterns, or standards," all while respecting the spirit of the corporate mission.

When I first read that definition of orbiting, I wanted to make a poster of it, turn it into a t-shirt, memorize it, and post it on my office wall. It is the essence of so much of what I've devoted myself to over the last two decades as I have tried to stretch myself and others to explore the promise and possibility beyond "accepted models, patterns, and standards" in education. My passion is to look to what is possible, not just to cling to past successes or ingrained educational practices.

When we look to what is possible, we discover educational vistas that are new to us, and we infuse our communities and our own minds and with passion and creative energy, but we can choose to do so without abandoning the educational establishment. We find ways to breathe creativity into these institutions, maintaining a deep love and respect for the important missions that drive many of our schools and learning organizations. We commit ourselves to helping reveal how that shared and valued mission can be expanded and enhanced through creative and innovative endeavors.

28

When to Reform and When to Start from Scratch?

"You never change things by fighting the existing reality. To change something, build a new model that makes the existing model obsolete." — R. Buckminster Fuller in *Critical Path*

I've had this conversation with dozens of people who are passionate about new possibilities for teaching and learning. Is it better to try to reform the school or learning organization where you find yourself, to find a place that is already a great fit for your values and beliefs about education, or to join the few entrepreneurial ones who start something new? There is no definitive answer to such questions. So many factors come into that type of decision, not the least of which has to do with discerning one's calling at a given time in life.

At the same time, I've witnessed enough learning organizations to see that massive, transformational changes in the way a community imagines education rarely come from reforming existing schools. Even when one is starting something new, it is common to be drawn gradually (or quickly) back into standard traditions and practices. That is because those running it have the imprint of past practice. Even when we don't intend to do so, we easily revert back to what others have done and how they have done it. It is the collective school ecosystem that persistently pulls us toward the norm. What started as a truly alternative project-based learning high school gets pulled into traditional practices as high school students want to take more AP and dual-credit classes to get a head start on college. Alternative school programs within a traditional school become restrained by shared resources, standard schedules, and other leaders who don't fully embrace or understand the importance of autonomy. Well-meaning teachers over-plan and over-structure self-directed schooling out of self-doubt or fear that students really can't or will not self-organize. The traditional nature of the next level of schooling begins to drive schools toward normalcy. If this happens with learning organization startups, how much more does it happen when one tries to reform an existing entity?

Then we have the Bucky Fuller quote, suggesting that fighting against the existing system is less likely to produce new and promising possibilities as much as independently pursuing those new possibilities. I read this to suggest that our energies are better focused on nurturing and actualizing promising possibilities than on fighting against existing realities. This can happen in existing organization or by creating new ones. It happens when teachers, leaders, or innovators opt not to be drawn into the drama or dysfunction around them (easier said than done, I know). It happens when an innovator embraces a promising practice and throws herself into making it a reality. Then she shares it with those who are willing and interested in learning more. It happens when an edupreneur ventures out to start something new and distinct from the norm. It happens in the smallest or simplest practices as well as grand and complicated ones.

The last part of the quote, about making the existing model obsolete, is probably where I might differ from Fuller, especially in education. When it comes to education, there tends to be much more convergence than obsolescence. MOOCs don't replace higher education. They get assimilated. Online learning doesn't make face-to-face learning obsolete, but it creates a massive blended-learning movement. The same thing is true for many emerging models. When it comes to education, there is room for many competing, complementing, and cohabitating models.

Nonetheless, for an innovation to take root, it needs its own space, its own soil, perhaps a very different type of soil than what works for the existing model. As I see it, that soil consists of freedom from most (or all) existing policies and procedures, room for a fair share of autonomy, and the ability to establish its own metrics and measures for progress and success. It needs room to tell its own story in its own way, and then leave it to others to decide whether they prefer the new or the existing model. Anything else is judging the quality of a rose by comparing it to an oak tree.

This is a difficult but important question for the educational leader and innovator. Sometimes you find yourself in an organization that creates freedom and space for true innovation. Sometimes you are able to help create that space. Sometimes you are the innovator who finds it challenging, even overly inhibiting, to pursue that mission-minded innovation that haunts and inspires you. In such times, it is important to consider deeply and candidly whether it is wise to pursue reform from within, to find another organization that better aligns with your vision and is willing to support it, or to venture out on your own, joining those few but important people who start new schools and organizations.

29

The Educational Entrepreneur's Code

Over the past several years, I've devoted much of my research to understanding entrepreneurial and innovative endeavors in the education sector. I've followed educational technology startups, emerging educational consulting firms and services, new forms of schooling (such as game-based, project-based, self-directed, personalized learning, and so on), the growth in MOOCs, the continually growing movement toward blended learning, and various types of one-to-one programs including bring-your-own-device (BYOD) schools. In many of these efforts there is an entrepreneurial spirit at work. There is a drive to create, influence, improve, innovative, design, and help. The motives are as diverse as the people who initiate these efforts.

As I like to point out, we are living in the Wild West era of education. Life in the western half of the United States during its formative years was interesting to say the least. We call those times the Wild West for a reason. There was risk, uncertainty, exploration, conquest, adventure, the shaping of new communities, and no small amount of merging (and sometimes clashing) passions and values. Rules were challenged, broken, and sometimes nonexistent.

Similarly, these are interesting times in education, regardless of anyone's assessment of its current state. There is experimentation and expansion, risk and uncertainty, and no small amount of clashing passions and values.

However, to carry the metaphor a little further, the Wild West was not a blank slate. It was not as if every person who came to live on the frontier abandoned all their prior beliefs and values. While some of those beliefs and values changed or were challenged, others continued to serve as guides through the new adventures. I contend that this fact is good and important.

Beliefs and values matter, and if educational entrepreneurs are the adventurers leading the way into the frontier of this digital age, then I suggest that we strive to maintain a few ground rules. Here are a few to get us started. I like to think of these principles as the foundation for "The Educational Entrepreneur's Code."

Pursue Social Good

Educational entrepreneurship is a subcategory of social entrepreneurship, which seeks to address social needs, problems, challenges, and opportunities. It is about pursuing social good. When it comes to building partnerships with educational entrepreneurs and merging educational businesses, the people who engage with them—whether educators, learners, or parents—must hold such organizations accountable. If entrepreneurs choose to do business in the education sector, then I argue that they should be held to a high standard. We must challenge these organizations to articulate their missions and explain to us how they see their products and services as providing social good.

Be Informed About Educational Research

Can you imagine a pharmaceutical company creating medical products without hiring and consulting with medical experts? Similarly, companies and consultants serving in the education sector must strive to be informed, if not extremely knowledgeable, about current and emerging research in the field of education.

(As a quick aside, I could say the same thing about educators and leaders of educational organizations, but unfortunately, I meet some educators and leaders who spend little to no time staying informed about current and emerging research in their field.)

Consulting with and hiring experts in the field certainly helps, too. Consider companies that promote educational software that promises to enhance learning and improve brain function. There is a huge difference between such products on the market. Some of these companies consult with and even have a staff of educational psychologists, neuroscientists, and educators. Others just use the word "brain" as a marketing tool, but with no actual insight into the research. We need more of the former.

Keep Student Learning and Benefit as a Core Value

Anyone in the field of education knows that education itself can be political. However, the reason that learning organizations exist is to help students learn. All educational companies and consultants should commit to designing products and services that ultimately benefit learners.

If a company's product is meant for teachers, then how does it help teachers help students? If it is a product or service marketed for schools or districts, how does the service or product help promote a chain reaction of events that eventually leads to improved conditions, services, or learning for students? The answers to these questions might even mean that we choose not to provide a particular service or product even if staff members are clamoring for it, unless the company delineates a clear vision for how its product or service ultimately benefits students.

Similarly, it is fairly easy for a company to create products that ride on the coattails of the latest policy or regulation. These products can be useful, but social entrepreneurs should still be called to communicate a clear understanding of how their product or service will deliver real and significant benefits for learners.

Innovation sometimes involves risk, but ethics demand that we persistently strive to minimize risk to the end users, which in this case is the learner. We endeavor first to do no harm, and this requires that we consider the potential affordances and limitations of a given product or service.

Be Transparent and Avoid the Dishonest Hard Sell

Financial transparency is important, of course, but transparency about the limits and benefits of a product or service is even more important. While it can be tempting to create a marketing plan that describes a product or service as if it were one of the top ten most important elements of a person's education, such is rarely the case.

What's even worse are marketing campaigns for educational products and services that seek to sell by conjuring guilt or fear. We don't need guilt and fear any more than we need educational products that are sold to make the buyer feel cool or trendy. What we need are educational products and services that truly benefit learners.

We need educators and educational leaders who are given the time, resources, and respect to weigh their options and choose what is best for their organization and the learners in their organization. Ethical educational entrepreneurs strive to provide this time and respect, and they do not seek to sell at all costs.

This principle of transparency applies to schools as well. I've yet to find a school that is a great fit for each and every student. Be honest about what your school does and doesn't do well.

Contribute to an Open and Collaborative Educational Ecosystem

As I mentioned earlier, to do business in the education sector is to be part of the educational system, and such participation calls for a shared commitment in the pursuit of social good. Yes, businesses compete with one another. Schools sometimes compete with each other. However, the end goal of education is not financial gain. Every organization that chooses to do business in the field of education is part of that field and has the opportunity to contribute to an overall ecosystem of products, services, and organizations that, as much as possible, looks for win-win solutions that ultimately benefit the learners. There are wonderful examples of this collaborative spirit in startup communities around the world, in the open source movement, and as shown by emerging partnerships between and among diverse learning organizations.

30

A Bad Habit Worth Keeping: Debunking Our Own Ideas

When it comes to new ideas, I have a bad habit that I intend to keep. I debunk my own ideas. At least I try. I encourage you to do the same thing.

An idea that doesn't hold up to a good debunking has questionable value. I might spend weeks or months unpacking a new educational idea. During this time, I'm likely to research it, experiment with it, and socialize it. When I share the idea with others and it is under scrutiny, that is when the most important work begins. Any idea that can't hold up under critique isn't an idea worth spreading. This doesn't mean that we need widespread consensus to move ahead. Great ideas can be unpopular. That may speak to their lack of marketability, but it doesn't speak to their truth and value. As Henrik Ibsen is credited with saying, "The majority is always wrong; the minority is rarely right."

Even when we decide to devote significant time to an idea, I'm convinced that the nobler path is to subject it to critique persistently. I'd rather abandon a wrong idea after a decade than persist with it for a lifetime. Sometimes we conclude that an idea is downright wrong, deeply flawed, or even destructive. More often, the practice of persistent debunking gives us perspective. It leads back to a phrase that you'll find throughout my blog (www.etale.org) and this book, "affordances and limitations." To the extent that an idea is a convention, technique, or invention, it has its benefits: things that it amplifies or things that it makes possible. It also has its limitations: downsides, things that it muffles, or things that it makes less likely or impossible. While we are tempted to turn a blind eye to the limitations of our favorite ideas, resisting that temptation is important. This kind of rigor allows us to refine the ideas. It is also what gives us the wisdom to discard others.

In 1949, Richard Weaver wrote what is now a classic text called *Ideas Have Consequences*. In it, Weaver warns of the dangers of egotism, making the self the measure of that which is valuable. With egotism, people become increasingly bent toward what benefits themselves instead of what is true. People stop valuing the pursuit of truth and find themselves content with fighting for and defending the preservation of the self or the group one feels a part of. The struggle becomes less about the affordances and limitations of an idea and more about the personal benefits and risks to the self of the idea. How does it help me? How does it support my goals? How does it assist our group or organization in achieving its goals or meetings its benchmarks? Power becomes more important than truth or goodness.

When this happens around educational innovation and entrepreneurship, we find ourselves defending educational ideas because they are ours or because they benefit us, not because they represent what is best for learners. We embrace ideas because we enjoy them more than because they help us to pursue truth, goodness, and beauty. K-12 teachers and university professors alike defend ideas that protect their preferred conditions or maintain the status quo. Educational leaders defend ideas that grant them influence. Entrepreneurs or educational business owners protect ideas that grant adequate or substantial financial gain. Professional organizations and educational associations defend their agendas. We establish an educational system where power and personal or affiliate gain trump the pursuit of truth and goodness. This is not to suggest that we should completely disregard self-preservation and financial gain, but a field like education is one that demands a higher calling along these other realities.

As I consider how to think and act in such a context, I remain convinced that there is value in continued innovation, but it must be innovation that is informed by humility, relentless in its analysis of affordances and limitations, and willing to sacrifice power and personal gain in the pursuit of truth and goodness in education, both in its aims and in its means.

Section V:
Knowing (or Creating) the Future of Education

31

Who Will Be the Winners and Losers in Educational Innovation?

In *Outthink the Competition: How A New Generation of Strategists Sees Options Others Ignore*, Kaihan Krippendorff describes four steps that occur repeatedly in warfare, sports, and business: 1. People develop rigid beliefs that only a certain way of doing things is best; they stop seeking better options. 2. Someone chooses an untrodden path and tries something outside of that common way. 3. The new strategy shows itself to be superior. 4. Others try to mimic the new practice, but it often takes them too long to catch up.

To what extent do Krippendorff's four steps apply in education? The author describes the steps as they show up in areas like sports, warfare, and business, where there are clear competitors. In those domains, it is team against team, army against army, or one business competing for the largest market share against a company within the same industry. While there is competition between learning organizations, I have difficulty recalling examples of where one learning organization completely dominated and shut down another, although one can make an argument for that happening in education businesses. I don't see struggles for dominance in education in the United States in either the K-12 realm or higher education, and I didn't think it was the case even when the University of Phoenix was at its peak enrollment of 600,000 students.

Krippendorff recommends a strategy of outthinking the competition instead of trying to overpower or outspend others. In education, despite the fact that there is little evidence of outright domination, we can see plenty of examples of attempts at overpowering and outspending. The fastest-growing online degree programs in higher education thrive not because they have identified new strategies that are unquestionably superior to online learning programs offered by others but because of the size of their marketing budgets.

When MOOCs first gained mainstream media attention, many argued that the MOOC movement could overpower and disrupt traditional higher education. However, to use Krippendorff's model, MOOCs would need to demonstrate superiority in an area that is central to the values of prospective students to do that. While MOOCs are certainly scalable and the price is right, they don't retain like traditional classes, lead to a valued credential (at least not typically or not yet), or prove to have superior academic results when compared to more traditional online or face-to-face courses. Instead, so far they seem to be serving a different purpose and a student population whose values are a far cry from those of students who gravitate toward more traditional learning organizations.

Others fear that micro-credentials and digital badges could overpower traditional models. I happen to be part of one of the first college degrees in the country that is built around competency-based digital badges, but I don't see evidence that our programs are going to shut down more traditional programs. Digital badges and micro-credentials have perceived value to some students, and I even contend that such programs are showing themselves to be superior to some more traditional feedback and grading practices, but they are not vastly superior, at least in terms of what people currently want. The same seems to be true about competency-based education (CBE) in general, although it is a relatively new movement. In the future, we may well find that CBE will have a larger and more widespread effect on learning than we might now expect.

Can we find an example of Krippendorff's four-step model anywhere in education? To do that, we may need to redefine what we mean by "the competition" in education. Perhaps the competition in education is not primarily among learning organizations. While schools do compete for students, prospective students have so many different needs and wants that there is currently ample opportunity for many schools to succeed, even if not all of them do. And while some futurists predict mass school closings on the college level in the next decade or two, so far there is questionable evidence that such a thing is taking place.

If, instead, we think of competition in another way entirely, we might be able to apply Krippendorff's model to education. For instance, Krippendorff applies his four-step model to a football game in the early 1900s when Notre Dame defeated Army by using the forward pass in a way that it had not been used before. Short rugby-like passes were commonly used back then, but Notre Dame took advantage of a change in the rules that year that allowed for passes of more than twenty yards. Notre Dame sent their man out for a long one and won that game by being the first team to adapt to the rule change. However, Army quickly caught on to the new strategy and adopted it in successive games, as did other teams, and long passes changed the face the game for good.

Such a model seems to be a more likely scenario in education. There are some interesting and potentially promising practices that may well show themselves to be superior to past practices. Options such as flipped instruction, alternatives to the letter-grade system, adaptive learning software for math instruction, data-driven decision-making in education, competency-based education for some educational purposes, and other trends can be seen as heralding the future. If one or more of these practices proves to be truly superior for certain purposes in education, those practices may well win out over practices that have outlived their usefulness. Yet, as long as organizations are willing to adapt, I don't expect to see a massive disruption in the industry as a whole that results in widespread closings.

Of course, I could be wrong. While my work and research are on the edges and take me frequently into new and emerging practices in education, I accept the possibility that I am, without realizing it, somehow stuck on Krippendorff's first step in one area or another, believing that there is only one acceptable way of doing things. If that's the case, I may at some point in the future be surprised by some other person, group, or organization that comes up with a model that proves to be unquestionably superior to the method or structure I am unconsciously clinging to. It's even possible that a new design will come from outside the formal field of education, catching many of us off guard and leaving us unable to respond or catch up fast enough. In general, though, I see plenty who are responding to innovations as they come along, at least on the organizational level.

Where I have more concern is on the individual level. I see some educators who insist on rejecting and ridiculing any and all educational changes and innovations that come along. Some don't even consider it worth their time to respond. Others laugh and mock, or they go the more civil route of trying to defeat it in public or intellectual discourse. Still others are on the attack, using words, legislation, and other clubs to beat down emerging practices, fighting to return to a past time or to keep a beloved practice. Those are the individuals for whom I am concerned.

I do not expect the latest innovation, technological or otherwise, to replace teachers anytime soon. I do, however, see that teachers who become skilled at using the best and most promising new practices will surely replace those teachers who resist and reject those practices out of hand. At this level and in instances where certain organizations refuse to adapt, perhaps Krippendorff's model of outthinking the competition will prove true in education after all.

32

Education Has Multiple Futures

Will MOOCs disrupt higher education? What about online learning or competency-based education? How will they affect K-12 and higher education? What about alternate credentials like the open badge movement? The more I engage in such questions, the more important it is for me to add adequate detail to better frame the conversation.

Education is a broad term. It includes early childhood centers, elementary schools, middle schools, high schools, community colleges, technical colleges, trade schools, research intensive schools, liberal arts schools, faith-based institutions, for-profit institutions, schools that focus on serving nontraditional or post-traditional adults, and many others. It also includes seminaries, graduate schools, distance learning schools, alternative colleges, and dozens of other types of institutions. To further complicate the questions, many education institutions include several of these distinctions under the same institutional name.

Programmatic Distinctions

Within these distinctions are various programs, professions, and disciplines, and the perceived benefits of each distinction vary. For instance, students of the performing arts may be less likely to benefit from online learning than will students of history. Alternate credentials will be less attractive to English majors in college than they will be to students in information technology. Similarly, MOOCs might hold less appeal for students who are in school for the social experience than they will for those who are interested in academics.

Student Goals and Motivations

A 2014 Parthenon Group report by Haven Ladd, Seth Reynolds and Jeffrey J. Selingo, "The Differentiated University," discusses the results of a survey of 3,200 prospective or current American college students. Rather than focusing on traditional demographic data, the survey examined the reasons for a student's interest in college. The authors were able to describe six distinct profiles of students: aspiring academics, coming of age, career starter, career accelerator, industry switcher, and academic wanderer. Each of these categories represents different motivations, goals, and aspirations, and each category embodies varied values about students' expectations and desires for their ideal experience in higher education. This perspective offers a clearer understanding about how and why the various distinctions—such as MOOCs, competency-based programs, digital badges, and online courses—might have higher or lower value to a given student.

Government, Community, and Business

While the profiles of learners have an effect on the future of education, so do external stakeholders. Government, communities, and businesses all have a stake in education, but what each one values differs from the others. Government tends toward a bias for economic development, while business is primarily interested in the development of a workforce that meets its varied needs, and the community's interests likely have more to do with how an institution affects quality of life. These descriptions are general and likely far too broad, but they illustrate the fact that a single future model of education is no more likely than it was in the past. Because learners, educators, and outside stakeholders have differing values about education, we continue to have many different types of education institutions today.

New Education Options

Among the external influences on education is the rapid growth of a new education industry. Look no further than CodeAcademy, General Assembly, Khan Academy, Udemy, new corporate training programs, and the overall increased access to free and open learning experiences online, for example. These new options in education appeal to a wide range of prospective learners, each with his or her own agenda and profile, and now all of us have more options than ever before. While such options may not soon overturn medical schools, they have already established alternate routes into some of the top high-demand jobs of the next decade such as software developers and system administrators.

Financial Factors

There are also important financial factors that affect education, especially higher education. Financial forces that can disrupt an expensive but non-exclusive college that depends heavily upon tuition will be different from those that can disrupt a public community college that is partly state-funded. Still other financial factors will affect an élite school with a massive endowment. There are schools with multiple sources of revenue and others that are almost entirely tuition-dependent. Some schools keep their doors open almost solely because of federal financial aid, while others have opted out of that model in favor of having the freedom to pursue different modes of education. These same distinctions exist among private and independent K-12 schools.

These financial factors heavily influence a particular school's receptivity to innovation. For instance, a school that is dependent in large part upon state funding will very likely not be in any hurry to adopt an innovative approach to American education, as it must first deal with a mountain of regulations and bureaucracy to do so.

With financial support comes regulation. With regulation comes restrictions on when, if, and how you can innovate.

The Need for Nuance

I don't mean to suggest that education as a whole will not be influenced by educational innovations. There is a long and clear history of innovation's effect on education. At the same time, I suspect that our conversations about the future of education will benefit from a more nuanced choice of words. I have been as guilty as others in making broad and general comments about the future of education with regard to emerging innovations. While such comments, including some I've read in *Inside Higher Education*, *The Chronicle of Higher Education*, and elsewhere, make for interesting conversation, they don't add depth and nuance, and they fail to give us tools for clarity in thinking about how to prepare for the future.

The Reality

The reality is that there is not just one future of education. There are multiple futures. Certain trends will unquestionably have large-scale influences, but even with that fact, the future of education is a varied one. As long as there are different people with difference philosophies, there will be different futures for education. As long as there are different needs and contexts, there will be different futures for education. And as long as there are different leaders and innovators in the field of education, we are looking at a future of education characterized by differentiation and variety.

33

What Can Educational Innovators
Learn from the Rise of Craft Beer?

I follow the news feeds on topics like entrepreneurship and startups, but I generally focus on news related to the education sector. Recently, however, a different type of headline caught my attention, one written by Drew Marshall in a 2014 *Washington Post* article: "What Your Company Can Learn from the Rise of Craft Beer."

I don't even drink beer, but something about that title caught my attention. The article writer explained that craft beer sales have increased by 17.2 percent while overall beer sales have dropped by 1.9 percent. What makes the difference? The article went on to explain that craft beer makers don't merely imitate the competitive practices of the big-name beer companies, but instead show a spirit of cooperation with other craft beer makers. They experiment with beer in new and creative ways; the companies are driven by founders who have a true passion for the product; and the industry as a whole is looking ahead.

I couldn't help but notice that the implied lessons in that article could also apply to those who are breaking new ground in the education sector, whether with new education startups or with innovative school models. While I do not see schools as standard businesses, they are organizations. As such, there are plenty of lessons that we can learn by looking at different types of organizations, applying those lessons to the field of education.

Do More than Imitate the Big Names

Education is full of imitation. In the higher education sector, there is a history of organizations that strive to be like Harvard, Stanford, or another of the élite schools. In the K-12 sector, there are private schools that do little more than imitate the practices of the public schools but with varying levels of exclusivity. Also in the K-12 sector, we see schools constantly striving to do and be what is trendy at the time, sometimes aided by the force of mandates. Additionally, I've seen schools of education in some universities that focus more on state policies and mandates than on any of the current research or cutting edge developments in the field.

Among education startups I see some of the most innovative work, but even there we witness people wanting to be the next [fill in the blank]. There is nothing wrong with learning from other organizations (I certainly do that all the time), but there is so much need and opportunity in taking the road less traveled in the education sector. The largest organizations are not always the best ones to imitate, and some truly compelling and promising innovations in the education sector are difficult or unlikely to scale. Taking the lesser-traveled route might not captivate venture capitalists, but there are plenty of other workable funding models. Innovating in education is about more than finding a blue ocean strategy. It is about breaking new ground, exploring new possibilities, and creating new opportunities. As Todd Henry wrote in *The Accidental Creative: How to Be Brilliant at a Moment's Notice*, "Cover Bands Don't Change the World." If we are going to nurture a craft-beer equivalent in the education sector, both with startups and schools, that calls for original work, or at least creative twists on existing work.

Embrace a Spirit of Cooperation with Other Education Startups and Innovative Schools

Years ago, when I conducted a study of the traits of leaders in innovative schools, cooperation was a quality that stood out instantly. It didn't take a formal study to see that people who were starting educational schools and other education startups loved to share and collaborate, and they were often quick to help others who wanted to do something similar.

They embraced a spirit of openness, recognizing that they were doing the work they were doing for something more important than prestige and financial profit. They didn't necessarily ignore the importance of financial or competitive realities, but they were driven by a vision that, regardless of the finances and competition, led them to lend a helping hand, share, cooperate, and nurture a broader community around their work.

We see this quality in innovative charters, magnet schools, private schools, and amid certain groups like democratic and problem-based learning schools, and elsewhere. I'd love to see this spirit expand.

Experimenting with Education in New and Creative Ways

The article pointed out some interesting experiments coming from craft beer makers. You can find chocolate beer, hot pepper beer, and other flavors such as oyster, key lime, peanut butter, banana, and about a hundred more. I'm pretty sure there isn't a widespread market for an oyster stout, maybe not for any oyster beverage. Yet, amid these experiments are some truly promising discoveries. That same thing is true in the "craft education" marketplace. As I've written before, I do not advocate thoughtless experimentation on children. Yet, given that the product, service, or environment meets some of the basics (even if it remains debatable), there is ample room to experiment, especially when we invite the learner(s) into the experimentation, making it part of the learning experience.

Passion-Driven Work

I don't want to confuse emotion with passion. While some definitions of the word "passion" focus on emotion, I think of it more in terms of conviction and drive. What I'm thinking of here goes far beyond a specific personality type. This is about the extent to which people truly care about what they are doing and why it matters. They are "true believers," and while they might encounter many challenges, they find joy in their work, and they are driven to be a difference-maker. In the education sector, I contend that work must be driven, in some way, by a desire to do something of significance that ultimately and genuinely benefits learners. I sometimes call this the "Mr. Rogers Mindset" and I consider it a nonnegotiable mindset for educational innovators.

Looking Ahead

Tradition has its benefits, but as traditions become more established, there can be a resistance to ongoing exploration of how to respond or adapt to what is new. The author of the article on craft beer explains that craft beer makers are more apt to welcome looking ahead and be open to embracing the new than is the broader beer industry. The same is true for educational innovators, who must work through or look behind cliché statements about new developments.

I'm still surprised when I run across people who assume that using technology is somehow less personal than the old ways. Technology can be impersonal, but it doesn't have to be. Others resist any number of developments because they have an opinion about them, but they have not truly investigated the affordances and limitations of those developments. Looking ahead is not about adopting every new development or buzz word, but it is about keeping our eyes open, being really curious, and allowing ourselves to explore new developments without making our minds up before we begin.

The "craft beer" equivalent in education is alive and well. We see it in new education startups, open source projects, new school starts and restarts, even in those areas with long traditions like publishing and higher education. These movements are not trying to become the next [fill in the blank], but instead leaders drive them with a passion for their product or service, leaders who are cooperative, forward thinking, and experimenting in interesting and sometimes unusual ways. Many of their innovations are unlikely ever to become mainstream in education, but that is not always the point. They meet needs of a niche audience and they support a vision of education that is not fixed, one that realizes that a variety of options is superior to universal standardization.

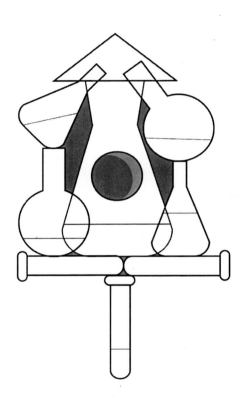

34

Building Educational Birdhouses

What does it take to build a birdhouse? How about an educational birdhouse?

These are questions I've asked several audiences, as it's a helpful way to illustrate the role and importance of educational innovation. It is an unusual question for an audience of educators or educational leaders. The strangeness serves to capture their attention, even their curiosity.

I prime the responses by showing a picture of an ordinary birdhouse, and the replies are always the same. It takes wood, a hammer, nails and/or screws, and a drill. The tools are standard, as our vision of birdhouses is often standard.

Then I ask again: How do you build a birdhouse when none of those resources are available, or if you want to take advantage of other resources? I show a second slide, this time with a wide and wild range of designs. There is the discarded cowboy boot with a hole drilled in the side. There is the dried gourd. There might be a clay birdhouse or one made of a recycled can or bottle. Now, looking at these options, what does it take to build a birdhouse? This shift of images opens eyes to the possibilities in our thinking about education. What does it take to build an educational birdhouse?

The ultimate mission is largely the same: to build a structure that serves as a house for birds. Lose that mission-minded focus and you can build wonderfully creative contraptions, but they don't accomplish a compelling mission. Similarly with an educational birdhouse, it is valuable to start with the mission, vision, values, and goals. Then we can assess how to best build that structure. With such an approach, innovation becomes one of our greatest allies. As you've hopefully considered throughout the essays in this book, without a mission-minded focus, innovation can quickly move us toward chasing shiny things, the bells-and-whistles approach to educational entrepreneurship.

Now consider the role of policy and practice in education. If we start with the assumption that you build a birdhouse only one way, and that way requires a hammer, nails, drill, wood, and the like, then we risk losing out on some wonderfully creative and powerful opportunities. This happens all the time in education. We crave clarity or a simple recipe, and we start with too many assumptions about what education should look like, and so we build something that is largely the same as what we had before.

Then we establish policies, regulations, and standard practices that force others into the same type of educational birdhouse building. When we see rich and creative alternatives, the educational equivalent of the repurposed cowboy boot, we view them with doubt and suspicion. Or sometimes we try to regulate those groups into more standard practice. If that fails, we label it "alternative," unrealistic, and not scalable, or we use some other phrase that allows us to dismiss it as the exception to the rule that we say should dominate our work in education.

During *Teacher Entrepreneurship Week* in the summer of 2015, Steve Hargaddon interviewed several educators, and I was one of them. He asked each of us to share a definition of teacher entrepreneurship, and I broadened the definition I gave to include educational entrepreneurship: "Teacher entrepreneurship is a creative, radical, passionate, mission-minded pursuit of the unconventional."

Why creative? Entrepreneurship is creative because it is usually about coming up with an idea and turning it into a business. Ideation is a key component of an entrepreneur's mindset. The same is true for educational entrepreneurship.

Why passionate and mission-minded? That's because entrepreneurship in the education sector is, as I've mentioned several times in this text, a form of social entrepreneurship. It is missional in nature; it is about using the tools of the entrepreneur to bring about a social good. To be a teacher entrepreneur is to have an educational mission and to be both passionate about and committed to that mission.

What about radical and unconventional? These qualities bring us back to the birdhouse analogy. We get stuck in one way of thinking. If we could find a way to look at things differently, we could see a world of solutions and find better ways of doing things.

Many of the challenges in education are more difficult to address because of the policies, practices, regulations, rituals, and standard practices that we have embraced. These policies and regulations were usually added for good reason, but over time they have lost their value. They either serve no purpose now or they have become outright obstructions to addressing some of the greatest challenges and pursuing some of the most promising opportunities.

There are so many current examples. There was the "aha" moment about competency-based education that leads to great opportunities, but the expansion of that concept is stunted because outside agencies can't figure out how to regulate it. Online learning increases access and opportunity in amazing ways, but in higher education, shifting and even competing standards and regulations from various agencies create major challenges to providing learning in online formats. Personalized learning serves diverse students, but old ways of thinking—about education as an act of mass distribution of content or standard instruction for all—hold that trend back. Individual teachers encounter students with distinct needs and try to personalize the learning experience only to get their hands slapped by administrators or others because they ventured into a nonstandard practice or tried to do something that doesn't fit the existing model or framework.

Because of these hindrances, schools, teachers, students, and the world as a whole lose. Schools lose out on being as effective as they could be, and they lose amazing and innovative teachers who too often leave for environments where they can better engage their entrepreneurial inclinations. Students lose out on great learning experiences. The world loses out on gifts and abilities not nurtured or discovered among students during their school years. Restricting ourselves to a single, standard approach to building educational birdhouses squelches potential in organizations, individuals, even entire communities and cultures.

At the same time, we are in a promising era in education because more people are trying new and unconventional approaches to building educational birdhouses than at any other time in history. Experiments are being conducted within the most regulated realms, and other important experiments in education are incubated safely beyond the influence of restrictive policies and regulations. This expression of creativity and ingenuity is promising. It is a strength of modern education.

Now our task is to help it spread. Let's help nurture a world of crazy, unconventional, diverse, and mission-minded educational innovations. Let's resist the temptation to build a massive yard full of standard educational birdhouses, letting go of the temptation to centralize and overly standardize. Let's value diversity and creativity and accept the fact that learning conducted in these ways will not be as easy to quantify as education structured in the standard way. Let's usher in a new era of building educational birdhouses. It's time.

35

Light bulbs and Moonshots

In 1876, seeking respite from the notoriety his earlier inventions had brought him, Thomas Edison established a laboratory in Menlo Park, New Jersey, where he went on to develop some of his most important inventions. I'm ready for some Menlo Park laboratories to benefit the education sector.

Learning from Thomas Edison

Thomas Edison's first patents focused on Samuel Morse's invention, the telegraph. Edison developed different types of telegraphs and installed tweaks and twists on this already-existing innovation. His work was initially iterative, largely a set of sustaining innovations that improved upon instead of disrupting existing products. He added new features and capabilities that improved upon past models.

Edison started his career by working as a telegraph operator. He wasn't inventing them, just using them, getting to know this new technology and field of work. As he became more familiar with that industry, he began to discover some of its problems and its limitations. He let his mind wander, imagining some of the possibilities and the opportunities, and out of those ruminations his own innovations began to arise.

He moved to New York City and eventually started a company that focused on selling some of his early innovations and creating new ones. With these early innovations, he generated the revenue to explore even more inventions, each one leading to the next, one brilliant innovation after the other.

But when he established his Menlo Park Laboratories in nearby New Jersey, his work really took off. Edison's lofty aspirations in those days aimed for a minor innovation every ten days and a major one every month or so. Gifted people came from all over the world to work together in those labs; they wanted to be around this innovative mind.

Thomas Edison was a human being, and he had flaws as well as strengths. He was brilliant at times, not so brilliant at others. When he was a child, for instance, he didn't speak until he was four, at which age he burst forth with an avalanche of questions about how things worked. His school teacher became so frustrated with young Edison's incessant questioning that he labeled him "addled," prompting his devoted mother to withdraw him from school and teach him herself.

And yet, Edison did something phenomenal. He pulled together a community of kindred souls around the spirit of innovation, and together they generated numerous patents that altered the face of American life, among them not only the phonograph and the light bulb, but also the world's first practical centralized power system.

In retrospect, though, we can see Edison's work as transformative in a more fundamental way. Power shifted during that time from the politicians in the capitol buildings to the groundbreakers and innovators whose inspirations flowed through the country's patent offices. A distinctly American mindset was being formed, and it had little to do with politics. The United States Patent Office became a central hub for innovations that dealt with everything from minor inconveniences to large societal issues, and Americans began to think of themselves as a people who could innovate their way through just about any challenge.

The First Moonshot

On May 25, 1961, President John F. Kennedy gave a speech to a joint session of

Congress. In that speech, President Kennedy shared a vision for the entire nation to rally around, that within a decade the United States would send a person to the moon and bring him back safely. His speech started the clock ticking for the world's first moonshot, and countless people ramped up their work to make that vision a reality. Some even died in pursuit of this goal. Nonetheless, like the inventers in Edison's Menlo Park Laboratories, the doers and dreamers persisted; they innovated, they experimented, they explored, they designed, and they planned.

On July 20, 1969, everything came together and the first person walked on the moon. "One small step for a man, one giant leap for mankind," said Neil Armstrong when he stepped from the landing pod onto the lunar surface. Then, as Kennedy had envisioned, the astronauts returned safely to Earth and thus the first moonshot was accomplished.

Now we use the term "moonshot" to describe comparable visions and innovations. Google uses it represent some of their more far-reaching research and development initiatives. In 2015, they sponsored an event that drew people together around "moonshots" in education. The term shows up in the blogosphere, throughout social media, and among startups with grand visions for changing an industry.

What Are Education's Moonshots?

Certainly there is a benefit in learning from and building upon traditions and experiences, and in fact many great moonshots and exciting innovations in the world are inspired by past innovations. Most innovations don't just appear out of nowhere. Innovators continue to build upon the accomplishments of those early inventors in Menlo Park, New Jersey, as well as later innovations, including explorations into space.

What are our moonshots for education today? What are yours? What are those compelling visions where your passions meet a real and potentially game-changing need in the education sector? And how do you begin to act upon that vision? How do you rally people around you as Thomas Edison and President Kennedy did?

Moonshots are about doing things that haven't been done before, or they have at least never been done in your part of the world or in your context. With a moonshot there is no clear path, no easy guide to follow, no one's footsteps before you. You are in new and uncertain territory, venturing into a new land where no one else has ever been.

It's Time for a Menlo Park Laboratory for Education

I'd like to suggest that to generate more moonshots, we need some more Menlo Park Laboratories in the education sector. We need little labs in K-12 schools and universities around the nation. We need edupreneurs who blend a spirit of innovation with a fervent commitment to high-quality education. We need to nurture space for more and varied school experiments and innovations within existing institutions. We need virtual labs of like-minded educators in partnership with each other and working on shared innovations that tackle some of education's greatest challenges and pursue its greatest opportunities. We need to create policies and spaces that empower and reward strategic innovations. We need independent innovators dreaming and designing educational innovations that matter. We need educators and educational leaders who invite learners into helping design educational innovations and create the future of education for themselves.

Edison's light bulb and Kennedy's moonshot challenge both serve as inspirations for those of us working on the frontlines of educational innovation. They are reminders about a core part of American culture, one characterized by creativity, experimentation, innovation, and human agency. We will never be free from problems and challenges in education, but we can leverage our unique gifts, talents, and abilities to pursue missional innovations and improvements. It is my hope and prayer that the ideas in this book have provided you with a little more insight and inspiration in your pursuit of noble causes and missional innovation in education.

Suggested Reading

Chen, M., & Lucas, G. (2010). *Education nation: Six leading edges of innovation in our schools*. San Francisco, CA: Jossey Bass.

Christensen, C. M., Roth, E. A., & Anthony, S. D. (2004). *Seeing what's next: Using theories of innovation to predict industry change*. Boston, MA: Harvard Business School Publishing Corporation.

Cialdini, R. B. (1984). *Influence: The art of persuasion*. New York, NY: William Morrow and Company, Inc.

Cureton, L. M. (1971). The history of grading practices. *National Council on Measurement in Education, 2*(4), 1-8.

Diamandis, P. H., & Kotler, S. (2015). *Bold: How to go big, create wealth, and impact the world*. New York, NY: Simon & Schuster, Inc.

Durm, M. (1993). An A is not an A is not an A. *The Educational Forum, 57*(3), 294-297.

Furr, N., & Ahlstrom, P. (2011). *Nail it then scale it: The entrepreneur's guide to creating and managing breakthrough innovation*. Lehi, Utah: NISI Publishing, LLC.

Gardner, H. (2004). *Changing minds: The art and science of changing our own and other people's minds*. Boston, MA: Harvard Business School Publishing Corporation.

Henry, T. (2011). *The accidental creative: How to be brilliant at a moment's notice*. New York, NY: Portfolio/Penguin.

Johnstone, B. (2003). *Never Mind the Laptops: Kids, Computers, and the Transformation of Learning*. New York, NY: iUniverse, Inc.

Krippendorff, K. (2012). *Outthink the competition: How a new generation of strategists sees options others ignore*. Hoboken, NJ: John Wiley & Sons, Inc.

Ladd, H., Reynolds, S., & Selingo, J. J. (2014). The differentiated university. Boston, MA: The Parthenon Group.

Lewis, C. S. (1944). On the reading of old books. (Originally published as the introduction to a book by Ruth Penelope Lawson, now made available as a stand-alone.) http://www.theelliots.org/Soapbox2008/OntheReadingofOldBooks.pdf.

MacKenzie, G. (1996). *Orbiting the giant hairball: A corporate fool's guide to surviving with grace.* New York, NY: Viking.

Marshall, D. C. (2014, December 19). Small business advice: what your company can learn from the rise of craft beer. *The Washington Post.*

Postman, N. (1992). *Technopoly: The surrender of culture to technology.* New York, NY: Alfred A. Knopf, Inc.

Robinson, K., & Aronica, L. (2015). *Creative schools: The grassroots revolution that's transforming education.* New York, NY: Viking Penguin.

Rogers, E. M. (1962). *Diffusion of innovations.* New York, NY: Free Press, a Division of Simon & Schuster, Inc.

Sahlberg, P. (2011). *Finnish lessons: What can the world learn from educational change in Finland?* New York, NY: Teachers College Press.

Schwahn, C., & McGarvey, B. (2012). *Inevitable: Mass customized learning: Learning in an age of empowerment.* CreateSpace Publishing.

Stewart, V. (2012). *A world class education: Learning from international models of excellence and innovation.* Alexandria, VA: ASCD.

Thomas, D., Enloe, W., & Newell, R. (Eds.). (2004). *The coolest school in America: How small learning communities are changing everything.* Lanham, MD: R & L Education.

Wagner, T. (2012). *Creating innovators: The making of young people who will change the world.* New York, NY: Scribner, a Division of Simon & Schuster, Inc.

Weaver, R. M. (1948). *Ideas have consequences.* Chicago, IL: University of Chicago Press.

Weldon, L. G. (2010). *Free range learning: How homeschooling changes everything.* Prescott, AZ: Hohm Press.

CPSIA information can be obtained at www.ICGtesting.com
Printed in the USA
BVOW04s0208020616

450422BV00029B/81/P